WHO'S IN YOUR HOUSE?

SETTING BOUNDARIES IN RELATIONSHIPS

Apostle Fritz Musser

WHO'S IN YOUR HOUSE?

SETTING BOUNDARIES IN RELATIONSHIPS

Apostle Fritz Musser

Published by Cosby Media Productions.
www.cosbymediaproductions.com
Cover art: Cosby Media Productions
Edited: Shelley Mascia
ISBN: 9781790446216

TABLE OF CONTENTS

Chapter One

THE FRONT PORCH

RELATIONSHIPS

There are a lot of people who have been in relationships and been deeply hurt by them. For many, they either continue being hurt and victimized, or they build walls to keep people at an emotional distance. Sadly, they miss out on developing good, healthy, lasting relationships and are left with only the negative and painful sides. The power of a healthy connection with others has long-term benefits and far-reaching impacts.

Having been in pastoral ministry for many years, I have dealt with a lot of difficult relationships: some of my own personal experiences, some that I helped with as a pastor/counselor, and many that I have observed during my ministry. Since relationships are valuable to my pastoral ministry, I discovered on my journey that I needed to come to a greater understanding of the dynamic and diversity of relationships. For a relationship to be pure, it must be void of the negative control and impure influence.

> *Furthermore, true wisdom is a necessity when it comes to navigating through relationships.*

I have had several, very difficult personal relationships, just like many of you. We all have our stories to tell. After these experiences, I prayed to God for understanding that would help me to navigate through the maze of broken, difficult, and diverse relationships, and that He would grant me insight and the ability to cope with the pain and confusion. The key, I believe, is to learn how to discern other people's pains and issues, and to strive for my own sense of wholeness both emotionally and spiritually. If you are comfortable with yourself, then you are much more likely to approach others inconsistencies without becoming a victim. Furthermore, true wisdom is a necessity when it comes to navigating through relationships.

Relationships can have a negative or positive impact, but are almost always necessary. Difficult people usually are placed in our life for personal growth and development. I have a friend who says, "God will allow difficult people in your life before He is about to promote you." In other words, there will be something you will learn through the struggle and frustration that will be valuable in making you a person that is more complete and Christ-like.

God's View

It is important for you understand that it is the will and intent of God that we have relationships and that most of those relationships flourish. You cannot live on an island. You cannot live life without risking the dynamic of what you will gain from all types of relationships. In order for you to be effective for God, you must enter into relationships with other people. After all, God want us to influence others to fulfill His divine purpose. You cannot leave it up to somebody else, while you remain closed for self-preservation. You will never be happy until you take that healthy, albeit risky step in connecting to others, to see the beauty of God bringing people together for much bigger purposes.

As believers, we are "the church", but we don't always understand the magnitude of that statement. Jesus said to Peter, *"Upon this rock I'll build my church and the gates of hell will not prevail against it."* (Mt 6:18) The church is the *Ecclesia* which means *"The Called Out ones."* We are the "called out ones" to do the will of God in these last days; to spread the good news of the Gospel; to take the message and the hope of Jesus Christ to all people. When we speak, the very truth of God and the power of God should flow through our lives. To do so, we must be in right relationship with God and others.

This speaking is not just preaching sermons from a church pulpit or teaching a small group Bible study; this is about a Godly connectedness where you can impact other people simply from a day to day relationship. This is where your relationships become empowered by the God in you, and you allow His presence over your life to bring out the best.

What About Being Hurt?

Everybody is concerned about avoiding being hurt, victimized, or taken advantage of. We quickly say, "What if someone hurts me? What if they reject me?" These questions and more resonate within us because of our own fear. We should never hold back from God's best for us because of unhealthy fear. Through this book I will explain that Godly wisdom will give you healthy control in relationships. Many people feel like they have been taken advantage of, but only because, they unknowingly allowed themselves to be taken advantage of from lack of discernment and wisdom. If you knew someone was taking advantage of you and to be protected emotionally, physically and spiritually to the point that it has little or no effect, would you be interested?

Once you know how to prevent people from taking advantage of you, and yet avoid building walls, you will understand the power of what God can do in others through you. God wants to use your relationships to influence and be influences. It works both ways. The key is knowing the right thing to do and walking in the right kind of protection that allows the relationship to be healthy, strong, and effective in the Kingdom of God. Your life will take on new meaning as you begin to see your relationships flourish and become healthy.

What We Need Foundationally

To discuss relationships, we have to begin with the most basic level of what relationships are all about: Wholeness. In 3rd John, verse 2 it says, *"Beloved above all else I want you to prosper and be in good health even as your soul prospers."* We have to make sure that we are healed and complete, and that we are standing right with God. Holding on to unhealthy fears can void the process. To prosper, our thoughts needs to be pure and submitted to the grace of God. We must learn to let go of our fears and trust God, to drop off the excess baggage we have been carrying. To do that, we must dare to trust God, exercise Godly wisdom, and take some strategic risks in relationships.

Will you never ever get hurt again? Unfortunately, people are not perfect and there will never be a perfect world where everyone will think and act just like you. You will be hurt, but the pain will be far less once you dare to risk through Godly wisdom. You will purposefully enter in to the relationship with Godly wisdom and understanding, along with an element of control. You will quickly understand that you can maintain and operate out of a pure heart.

David said, *"Create in me a clean heart, renew a steadfast spirit"* (Psalm 51:10). First, ask what is the potential purpose of this relationship. Are you connecting with them for what they can do for you? Be honest with yourself and know that relationships are not for self-serving purposes. Always check your motives. Are you in a relationship because it could potentially be a divine connection? Your heart will become your agenda, and a corrupt agenda will produce corrupt and difficult results, so purify your heart so your motives to corrupt end.

> *I call relationships like that, a "God hook up."*

Many times, people are in relationships for all the wrong reasons. Sometimes those reasons get exposed when it's too late and you already feel victimized by someone's impure agenda. You must always check your motive by continually looking at any indicators that there may be a one-sided agenda. Are you truly in the relationship for gains, rather than what you might have to offer, or better yet, what God might do through that particular connection? Godly connectedness always has a purpose much deeper and greater than what we could ever understand. I call relationships like that, a "God

hook up."

Learning From Our Mistakes

I cannot tell you how many people I have

talked to who have said, "I've built all these walls to

protect myself, and now after all these years, I am

trapped in my own prison." We take those past hurts

and mistakes, and we build walls to keep people from

getting in, but ultimately those walls not only keep

people from getting in, but they keep us from getting

out, and now we are imprisoned. We cannot afford to

build walls like this. It will cause wasted years of

unnecessary pain for you and others, because they

will never discover in you what you can't discover

within yourself. You are special in God's eyes and you

have much to offer, but most of the world will never

see it because of your unhealthy guarded control.

10

A good question to ask is, are you afraid of being hurt? Are you bitter because of what close friends have done to you? Are you still upset because of what somebody did to you years ago? Have you become the eternal victim? If this sounds familiar, then understand this important truth about relationships: Just as God never intended for you to be isolated and alone, He never intended for you to be beat up, wounded, and hurt in all or most relationships.

Starting Fresh

Ok, so you've made mistakes in the past. You're not alone, we all made mistakes. Now is the time for you to let God bring healing into your life. In I Samuel 30:6, David encouraged himself in the Lord. The Bible says he found strength in the Lord, his God. You are going to find your healing for long, healthy relationships. Find strength in God today and allow Him to bring that healing. Let Him dismantle the walls that you have built and have created out of self-preservation, which have always produced volatile and painful results. Realize the value of relationships and the value of connectedness that God wants to bring in your life and recognize the power of the relationship that God wants to bring to His church, the Body of Christ.

Since it is the will of God for you to have relationships with other people, walking in Godly wisdom is necessary. Proverbs 4:7 says, *"Wisdom is the principle thing, therefore, get wisdom."* One translation says, *"Wisdom is supreme."* It says that you and I are to *"get wisdom."* Wisdom is not the same as knowledge. Knowledge is acquiring information, but wisdom is the ability to handle the information. A lot of people confuse these two. It is possible to have knowledge and not have wisdom.

There are people who are blessed with a lot knowledge. Quite possibly, they have made a career out of it, but they lack the wisdom to take what they know and increase it 100-fold. Also, there are people who have very little knowledge, but they have a gift of wisdom to take what they do know, and to navigate that into great successes and blessings. You want to make sure that you have the wisdom of God to rightly handle what you know.

So, that is what wisdom is; the ability to rightly handle what you know. We all understand what it's like to do something that totally lacked wisdom and was born mostly out of raw emotions and feelings. We all know how it is to suffer the consequences of those things we said or did. To be wise in relationships and to manage your relationship properly is to avoid getting hurt and wounded so often that we avoid them altogether.

The power of God will cover what you say on a day-to-day basis when you trust in Him and walk in His ways. God can put power in your words and your words can positively impact others to move to the next level of life and God's will for them.

God can bring healing on the job just because you speak a word into somebody. When God gives you that word, He can bring healing in the marketplace, and in the streets. When you speak a fresh word from God out of your spirit, you can avoid getting caught up in clichés, religious phrases, or traps of saying the same thing over and over. You are actually asking God to use you on a daily basis.

Be Sharp, Stay Sharp

Proverbs 27:17 says, *"As I iron sharpens iron, so one man sharpens another."* Let me ask you–have you ever been "sharpened" by someone else? Have you had conversations with someone and found yourself stimulated to walk away and learn more? Conversely, how many people have you been around that have dulled your senses to the power and goodness of this life? If the Scripture says that we are supposed to sharpen one another, then the people you hang out with the most will affect you. I have a friend that says people are like elevators; they take you up or they take you down. If you want to grow in the things of God, make sure that you stay sharp in the things of God, sharp in your own relationship with Him and others, and sharp in the way you deal with others. Make sure that there are people in your life who sharpen you in the ways of God.

The House Analogy

One day, I was really having a hard time understanding why somebody would come into my life and then just walk out as if we never knew each other, or why someone would come into my life as a friend and leave a full-blown enemy. I found myself so frustrated that I asked God to please give me direction and understanding. I knew enough to say, "God, what am I doing wrong? Is it me?" rather than blaming everybody else. I also knew enough to say, "God, what am I doing that I allow people into my life to hurt me? It immobilizes me to that point that I am not effective for you?" God gave me the analogy of a house as He unfolded the process of all relationships.

In a house, you typically have a front porch or some type of landing at the front door, then a foyer, and some houses have a formal living room, some a

16

formal dining room, but all houses have a kitchen, some kind of a family room and, lastly, at least one bedroom.

When a person, for example a salesman, comes to your house and he comes to the front door of your house, do you automatically greet them and say, "Oh, it's so good to see you. Just come on in to the house?" Of course not, you never just openly welcome a stranger into your home; you have no idea who they are, and you certainly don't know them well enough to invite them into your personal space.

But this is what frequently happens. We openly welcome people into our life just because they seem nice. We move too quickly into a level of intimacy that is unhealthy and premature, when we should have kept them on the front porch and not let them into our homes at all.

WHO'S IN YOUR HOUSE?

Can you still be "friendly" with the salesman and keep him on the front porch? Absolutely. It doesn't mean that he cannot or will grow into a stronger friend. It just means that the relationship must be tried and tested.

This book is not intended for you to "interview" the people you come in contact with to assess where you might be with them based on this analogy. This is for your personal evaluative purpose only. I don't want people to go around saying, "Where am I in your life? Am I on the front porch?" This

> **But you don't invite them into your house, and certainly not to your bedroom.**

is not something you answer with someone else, because it is insignificant and mostly irrelevant to their personal journey or yours. They can be your "friend" and you can control how close, and how quickly, you let them into your life. They may want to be in your bedroom, the deepest level of intimacy in relationships, but they need to be on the front porch, and may remain on the front porch for a long time. They can still be your friend from that place. You can have a purpose-filled conversation with the salesman on the front porch and walk away saying, "He or she is a very nice person. We just had a great time talking to each other." But you don't invite them into your house, and certainly not to your bedroom. It sounds ludicrous to even think of such a thing, but in this analogy it happens all the time on the emotional, relationship level.

Also, please note that the term "intimacy" is used to describe the level of relationship that you would feel comfortable and safe to "bare your soul", not fearing that they would ever use it against you in any way.

David And Saul

Throughout this book we will be referring to the story of David and his relationship with Saul, the King of Israel. In I Samuel 16:19-22 tells us this:

19 *"Then Saul sent messengers to Jesse and said, 'Send me your son David who is with the sheep,' so Jesse took a donkey loaded with bread and skin of wine and a young goat and sent them with his son David to Saul."*

21 *"David came to Saul and entered his service. Saul liked him very much and David became one of his armor-bearers."*

22 *Then Saul sent word to Jesse saying, 'Allow David to remain in my service for I am pleased with him.'"*

Let us examine the dynamic of Saul's relationship with David. In verses 19-21, Saul sent for David and he liked him so much that he asked that

David remain as his armor-bearer. Just because somebody likes you does not mean you let them too far into your emotional and intimate life. You may say, "But they really like me a lot." Is that what life is all about? Is that what relationships are all about? Just because they like you does not mean that you trust them with everything you have. Verse 22 says, *"Then Saul sent word to Jesse saying, 'Allow David to remain in my service for I am pleased with him.'"* Saul said, *I am pleased with him.*

People can like you and things really look pure and connected at first, but it can change over time.

In the 17th and 18th chapters of I Samuel, David rises to prominence. Something happens in David's life and we see that he is accomplishing great works. He kills the giant Goliath with great success. The women are singing his praises. In fact, the people are even singing a song that says, "Saul has killed his thousands; David his ten thousands." Suddenly, Saul begins to change and is now jealous and suspicious of David.

This same dynamic happens in relationships all the time. People will enter relationship with you because you are accomplishing things, getting blessed, good things are happening in your life, you are popular, etc. Then they become jealous of you, and jealousy, if not dealt with, will have a negative effect on any positive advancement. Jealously carries with it a wicked form of character assassination. Where you were once so valuable to them, you are now the lowest form of life. It all happens over the course of time and revealing of the heart.

Changing Our Armor

In I Samuel 17:38 when David is about to go out and face the giant, Saul tried to put his own tunic on David and it didn't fit him. That's because it was designed for Saul. Some people will try to push their own agendas on you. But, like David, you need to boldly declare, "This doesn't fit. I've got to be the person that I am in Christ, not the person you are trying to force me to be." Some people will try to change you because they are thinking of you as the friend they want, with stipulations. They will try to change you into something that you should not be, by putting demands on you to meet their expectations, which are almost always unhealthy and damaging.

I Samuel 17:45-46 tells us this:

45 *"David said to the Philistines, 'You come against me with spear, and a sword, but I come against you in the name of the Lord'."*

46 *"This day the Lord will hand you over to me and I'll strike you down and cut off your head. Today I'll give the carcasses of the Philistine army to the*

birds of the air and the beast of the earth and the whole world will know that there is a God of Israel."

Do you see the power of the confidence that David has? This is the power and blessing of God on his life. It was because of God's blessing on David that Saul began to change. In I Samuel 18:9 we learn, *"Saul kept a jealous eye on David."* After all, don't you want to have friends who are happy when you get blessed? Those are the kind of friends you want, but Saul was suspicious of David. Verse 11 says, *"Saul had a spear and he hurled his spear saying to himself, 'I'll pin David to the wall.'"* Have you ever had friends do whatever they could to back you into a corner? It says, *"But David eluded him twice."* So, suspicion turns to rage, and rage turns to anger, and Saul tries to kill David with a spear, but David eluded him.

There may be times when you are in relationships and they begin throwing insults, accusations, and offenses at you at speeds similar to someone shooting at you with destructive force, and you must work to avoid their malicious, deadly impact, which can be painfully devastating. Words can hurt. The old saying, "stick and stones will break my bones, but words will never harm me" is not really true. Words can wound our spirit. When this happens, it is not the time for you to say, "That's it. I'm done. I'm never going to trust anybody ever again." Don't make an emotional, knee-jerk decision that you will regret. Remember, now is the time for you to ask for and trust in the wisdom of God.

Front Porch Friends

Let's go back to our house analogy. We are learning to be completely in control of our relationships. When you are the one who is in control,

you can decide how far and how fast others enter

your life. This is not about building walls or about

resisting and not having relationships at all. This is

about you walking in the wisdom of God and deciding,

like David had to decide with Saul, that there was

something that was not right. Something had changed

in Saul, he had become very jealous of David.

But you cannot be wise in relationships until you are in your own personal relationship with God, who fills you with wisdom and understanding.

Sometimes people will change in relationships and you may have already invited them in. This is when it's time to quickly push them back out to the

front porch. You may say, "But he's my friend." Yes,

they are still your friend, but with necessary

boundaries.

There is nothing wrong with a front porch friend. It doesn't mean they're not special or they're not important. They still have great value and feel connected as if they were deeper in their relationship with you. This is the reason they should never be told where they are with you because you have the control. You are the only one that needs to know. David trusted Saul and didn't see him for what he was at first, but he trusted him. But then he became wise to Saul's plots to murder him.

You can still trust and allow so much, once God gives you the wisdom. But you cannot be wise in relationships until you are in your own personal relationship with God, who fills you with wisdom and understanding. You cannot have Godly wisdom unless you have a healthy relationship with God, because He is the one who is going to give you discernment, spiritual discernment, and show you how to handle your relationships.

Once you have wisdom, you will know what to allow or disallow in your life.

Dealing With Scheming

Saul tried the spear approach, and it didn't work, so he resorted to scheming. Have you ever had friends who had impure motives and who were scheming against you because they wanted something out of you? Check out verse I Samuel 18:17.

"Saul said to David, 'Here is my older daughter Merab. I will give her to you in marriage. Only serve me bravely and fight the battles of the Lord,' for Saul said to himself, 'I will not raise a hand against him. Let the Philistines do that.'"

In other words, *"I am going to send him out to the wolves. I am going to make it tough on him."* Then in verse 20 that Saul agrees to give David his daughter, Michal, because Merab was already taken.

20 *"Now Saul's daughter Michal was in love with David and when they told Saul about it he was pleased."*

21 *"'I will give her to him,' he thought, 'so that she may be a snare to him and so that the hand of the Philistines may be against him.' So Saul said to David, 'Now you have a second opportunity to become my son in-law.'"*

In verse 25, there is an unusual wedding gift. It says, *"Saul replied; say to David, 'The King wants no other price for the bride than 100 Philistine foreskins to take revenge on his enemies.'"*

Saul's plan was to have David fall by the hands of the Philistines. Saul's plan is not God's plan. Now, we are left to choose, do I want Saul's plan (the plan of someone else) or God's plan? You ultimately have to work out God's plan for your life. You must be confident in God's plan. When you walk in His plan, Saul's plan can never interrupt what God has for you. God has a purpose for you and when you are walking in it, you will have the confidence that God is in control and not disconnected with what is going on. In all of His omniscience, God has a perfect plan and He has provided everything you need to discover the beauty of His plan.

What About Jealousy?

In I Samuel 19:1, Saul's jealousy brings him to the point where he actually hires assassins to kill David. .

Would you say that Saul is unstable? That's an understatement! I heard someone say years ago,

"Hurting people hurt people." Saul is a mess! He has allowed a lot of things into his thoughts that have fouled up his relationship with David and others as well.

What if your purpose in that person's life is to lead or coach them? You might think, "If I keep them on the front porch, I won't be able to effectively lead them." Says who? You can lead just as effectively on the front porch as you can in the kitchen. You can lead people wherever they are. In fact, based on your insight, you can lead them better, because you know how to keep them in the right place.

Saul is obviously at a point in his life where he needs help. Maybe he is frustrated from the years of struggling with Samuel. Maybe he is frustrated with the worthless people who opposed his reign. Maybe he was frustrated with the Philistines. No doubt, he was frustrated about a lot of things.

WHO'S IN YOUR HOUSE?

This is not to psychoanalyze Saul, but I'm telling you that there is something awry in this relationship and Saul probably has an over-inflated ego because he's been negatively impacted by that song proclaiming David's greatness over his, *"Saul has killed his thousands; David his ten thousands."* So now he focuses his attention on David's death. It's important to see that Saul started out liking David, but through a process of personal changes that he (Saul) had control over, he changed for the worse.

Let's get this straight, not everybody in your life will stick with you all the way. Some people are in your life for a reason, and some people for a season. There are some people who act strangely because of jealousy or other things that they are personally going through. Can you still lead them? Yes. You can still be effective in ministry because you have allowed an atmosphere that protects you in all the right ways.

Some skeptics will write you off as naïve, and you're setting yourself up to be hurt, because they know better. The problem is they don't trust anybody, so they never risk and will never enjoy the fruit of a safe, healthy relationship.

Let's look at David. David had a promise from God that he would be king. You have a promise over your life that the blessing of God is yours and that God has anointed you and the power of His Holy Spirit is in you.

Furthermore, David had already been anointed by Samuel. You have been anointed through the redemptive work of Christ. The Spirit of the Lord is upon you. He has anointed you to preach the good news! David dared to go into battle against Goliath and to initiate the defeat of the Philistines. The Israelites marched for 40 days, but they didn't do anything. Every time Goliath came out, they walked away. They did not attack Goliath; they just went out and marched all day long. Goliath would come out and they would run.

Then David came on the scene. David had killed a lion and a bear. He had experienced good success, was confident in his relationship with God, and he wasn't going to stand around while the Philistine defied his God. He refused to wear Saul's tunic because it didn't fit him. He decided to do what he felt like God was telling him to do, which always fits better.

A Turning Point

Early on, we see that Saul has an unstable temperament. Now it was becoming a matter of public knowledge. Meanwhile, David was becoming successful and gaining a lot of public support. You, like David, have a challenge to move into the will of God and sometimes when God elevates you, people will turn against you. Many people miss the mark in ministry and they give up because they can't handle the attacks from people who are hurting. Life and ministry is all about relationships and learning how we deal with them with Godly wisdom. I have seen people give up ministry altogether because people do not like them, or they have been hurt too much. In fact, in my early years of ministry, it was something I considered more than once.

Just realize that you are not necessarily here on to be liked or popular by all people. You are here to serve God and to seek first His kingdom (Matthew 6:33). You are here to be confident in your service to God because of who you are in Christ, and because of all that Christ has purchased for you to be prosperous and successful in the ways of God. Being liked is the by-product of serving God. If you are serving God, you will be liked by other people who connect with the God in you.

The ones who have weird agendas always stay on the front porch. If the salesman we illustrated earlier repeatedly comes back, you would not, out of disgust give in and say, "Oh well, come on in." That relationship still has to be tested, regardless of peer pressure. People are always going to come back and test the relationship. David was successful and he still was obedient to Saul. Saul was messed up and David was cool because David was confident.

If you are confident in yourself, and have walked in Godly wisdom, it does not matter what people do to you because you have not allowed them into the intimate places of your life, and God will not only protect you from harm, but He will reward you with the benefits of His "Holy Hook ups."

Testing

My father, who is a pastor and has been a great father and a faithful husband, said something in one of his sermons that shocked me and several others in the congregation. He said, "My wife knows enough about me that she could destroy me." I later understood what he meant because the person that you are intimate with knows all your weaknesses.

You do not want the people on the front porch to know all your weaknesses and struggles. What typically happens in relationships is that somebody comes into our life, they appear nice on the surface, and we just unload many of our weaknesses. We are risking without wisdom. You don't know what they might do with that information because they seem like a "nice" person. But what we don't see is whether they are on moral stable ground or have strong spiritual insight. We haven't been around them long enough to see if they have a strong ethical foundation, or that they just simply may not have the ability to handle our information.

I was once informed by a fellow minister: "I am a pastor struggling with alcohol." I was totally shocked, I did not know that the man had any problems with alcohol whatsoever. As soon as he let that information go, he followed up with, "Please don't tell anybody."

I said, "Why would I want to tell anybody that you have a problem with alcohol? I have no desire to tell anybody." He told me his deepest struggle, because he trusted me. He knew me well enough to trust that I would not gossip and would know how to pray for him and encourage him through his struggle.

Before you allow somebody into the place where you share your intimate details, you better make sure they are not a Saul because they may use what they know against you some day. It is not for me to use what I know against my wife or for her to use what she knows against me. We love each other and our relationship was tested before marriage, and refined in marriage that we love and accept each other for who we are. The relationship has been tested. Our intimacy is secure in our trust.

It would have been easy for David to lose faith in God's promise. It would have been easy for David to say, "Why am I going through all of this? God, what is this?" Can you imagine? I have talked to people who were a lot like David and they were saying, "Why am I doing all this? The kinds of things that I have put up with are unreasonable. Do you know what people are doing to me? Do you know what they're saying about me?"

When you are serving God, not everybody is going to be happy with what you are doing. I want you to notice what happens every time Saul attempts to harm David because there are people on the front porch who will attempt to bring harm to your life. Romans 8:31 says, *"If God be for me, who can be against me?"* Say that statement boldly, *"If God be for me, who can be against me?"* When God is on your side, then the right people are on your side and the people who are against you are the ones you wouldn't want on your side in the first place. Saul attempts to harm David several times, including pinning him to a wall with a spear.

> *Our emotions take us here quick if we're not careful, and we are considering fleshly, and emotional alternatives to a Biblical principle.*

Saul became aware that there was something different about David. It was God's anointing on David that H was with David. Don't you think that if Saul could see it, that David was probably aware of it?

Don't miss this critical point…God's anointing is on you! If others can see it, then you should see it as well. If others do not respect you, they do not respect God's anointing on you. That means they see your anointing, but they don't know how to handle it. They see your success, but they don't know what to do about it.

What was David's attitude while he was under attack? David never attempted to strike back at Saul. That is not what he was about. Your attitude towards relationships is critical in how you handle those relationships. If you have the wrong attitude, then the relationship will not be what it needs to be. A right attitude is critically important.

When we were growing up—one of our rules was that you turn the other cheek— but we used to jokingly say, "You turn the other cheek after you've hit them." Our emotions take us here quick if we're not careful, and we are considering fleshly, and emotional alternatives to a Biblical principle.

Humans automatically think of retaliating. I have argued with the voice in my head where somebody did something to you, or somebody said something hurtful and five hours later, you were still talking about what you wish you could have said to them. Right? "Boy, if I would have, could have, I would have said this. I should have said this. I wanted to tell them this and I wanted to let them have this," but it is not for us to retaliate. Leave vengeance up to God.

David had confidence in God. You and I stand in that same confidence with David. Therefore, I dare to risk in relationships. Will I get hurt? Of course, I will but I am not going to get hurt nearly as badly as I would have if the people who hurt me were in the bedroom or other intimate areas of my life, instead of on the front porch.

The Promise

David had the promise of God and that was all David needed to know. David's confidence was not in himself, but in God. When facing Goliath he said, *"You come to me with sword and spear. I come to you in the name of the Lord my God."* You and I do everything that we do in the name of the Lord, our God. David awaited the fulfillment of God's promise. Many times, we become impatient with the fulfillment of God's promise and we become frustrated that the enemies in our life keep us from fulfilling the promise. But God may use the enemies to advance you to the promise. God may have allowed you to go through some tough things, so He could get you to the place that He needed for you to move into His ultimate

purpose.

Now let's go back to David. In I Samuel 24 we

see that David has been living as a fugitive in the

mountains for years. He has been hiding from Saul,

but Saul has found him out, and come to destroy him.

Let's examine the scripture and explore strategies to

achieve the promise, and to walk in Godly

relationships.

Be careful whom you listen to.

In verse 9, when David's men arrived, David

said to Saul, *"Why do you listen when men say,*

'David is bent on harming you?' Why are you listening

to this?" The key here is to be careful who you listen

to in relationships and why do their words have an

effect on you?

In one of the first churches I was pastoring, someone came to me in my first few days and pointed out a person in the church that I had not yet met. This person pointed him out to me and said, "That man," as he pursed his lips and shook his head, "That man is nothing but trouble. Stay away from him." I pastored that church for two years. For the first six months, I was afraid to get within ten feet of that person. The last day of my two-year ministry in that church, that person that he criticized was my right-hand man and a loyal friend, and still is today. My last Sunday at that church, before moving to Atlanta, he handed me a note on a little scrap of paper as he and his wife hugged me as I was loading my car to leave. The note is still in my desk drawer today. He said that he counted the number of days that I had been at that church. He wrote, "I have prayed for you twice a day for 731 days." and he slipped it into my pocket. The same man that someone else said, "Stay away from him. He's nothing but trouble," became one of my best friends and supporters.

Some people will try to corrupt your relationships with others because they do not want you to succeed, nor do they want you to have vibrant, healthy relationships. Do not listen to everything everybody says about other people. In fact, remember this basic rule-of-thumb: if they are going to talk to you about everybody else, then they will talk to everybody else about you. Don't think that you're so special that they are not going to tell others what they know (or think they know) about you. They will, because they aren't mature or they are so disconnected from the redemptive work of Christ that wisdom is far removed from them. They are only capable of a counterfeit relationship that is built on shaky ground that never lasts.

46

Let the fear of God keep you from sinning

In relationships, you must let the fear of God keep you from being presumptuous and sinning. There are a lot of ways to go wrong in a relationship. Sometimes, I have been in relationships when I wanted (in my emotional mind) to punch people out. I wanted to call them and give them a piece of my mind. My dad once said that if you keep giving people a piece of your mind, sooner or later you are not going to have any mind to give! The Bible says, *"In your anger do not sin."* Make sure you fear God enough that you don't fall into sin's trap by doing something that will only bear bad fruit. You don't always need to defend yourself or try to show someone how tough you are by confronting them. Sometimes, you just need to let God be your defense and keep your sights forward on God, instead of looking back and dwelling on some noisemaker.

Appeal To Your Own Actions

In verse 11, David says to Saul, *"See my Father look at this piece of your robe in my hand."* David had cut it off. He said, *"I cut off the corner of your robe, but I did not kill you. Now understand and recognize that I'm not guilty of wrongdoing or rebellion. I have not wronged you, but you were hunting me down to take my life."* David is still not doing anything against Saul. He appealed to his own actions. *"Look at what I have done, I have not done anything to harm you."*

As long as you do not do anything, you will have nothing to apologize for. Do what it right and your life will defend itself. Stand with a peaceful calm and refuse to be motivated to out of control emotions and bad decision making.

Do not retaliate and return evil for evil

David says in verse 12, *"May the Lord judge between you and me and may the Lord avenge the wrongs you have done to me, but my hand will not touch you."* When my children were little, my son would hit my daughter and she would hit him back. Or she would do something, and he would retaliate. It happened with both of them. I would talk to them and say, "Now who started this?" Sarah would say, "Josh did." I would say to my daughter Sarah, "Well, what did you do?" "Well I broke his game because he was mean to me." I said, "Was that wrong?" She said, "Yes sir." Then I said, "Now who is wrong?" And they would both say, "We both are wrong." And I said,

"One of you could have stopped this and I would be disciplining only one of you and not both of you together. If one of you would have decided to act mature and give a calm, peaceful response, you would be free from any discipline right now."

Wouldn't it be better if God were dealing only with somebody else for what they did to you, instead of having to deal with both of you because you retaliated with intense, out of control emotion?

Let your character speak for itself

In verse 13 David states that the known character of a person should prevent others from questioning their motives. He says, *"As the old saying goes, 'From evil doers come evil deeds' so my hand will not touch you."* In other words, I am not an evil doer. Let everybody say, *"He would never do something like that."* Let your character speak for itself.

Take a place of humility

Make sure that you remain humble. Verse 14 says, *"Against whom has the King of Israel come out? Whom are you pursuing, a dead dog, a flea?"* You want to be humble, then just be humble. Pride makes you think that you have to perform and prove yourself to others to save face. Not if your character has already gone before you. It's better for you to be silent and have good character that calms the negative atmosphere, then to make noise and create more confusion.

Leave the justice up to God

Look at Verse 15, *"May the Lord be our judge and decide between us. May he consider my cause and uphold it. May he vindicate me by delivering me from your hands."* Leave justice up to God. When you are in the right relationship with somebody, you want to make sure you have discernment and the wisdom of God in that relationship. Do not even think about acting out of emotion. Don't act on what you feel because typically what you feel at first will not be right. Act on the wisdom that God gives you and trust that wisdom. Say to yourself, "What is the smart thing to do in this relationship?" Or you can say, "What would Jesus do?" Make sure that, in all circumstances, you remain upright and pleasing to God. That way, you do not have to apologize for anything.

The Bible says in Romans 12:18 (NLT), *"Do all that you can to live in peace with everyone."* I used to think that was a contradictory statement, but I came to understand it in the right context. It does not say that as far as it is concerned with you, that everybody should be at peace with one another. It says that you should be at peace with them. They may not be at peace with you, but as far you are concerned, you should be at peace with them. Trust the wisdom of God and trust what is right. If you are in the peace of God, then they cannot move you because it's a vital part of your character.

People will try to get into your life. They will try to get closer to you, but you have to make sure that you have tested the relationship to see what their motives are before you allow them into other, more intimate areas. Friends can stay on the front porch and still be friends for a long time.

This is about what kind of a friend you are. Are you a real friend? Do you care about that person? That's all they know, you are their friend. But as far as you are concerned, they are still on the front porch.

Exclusive Company

As we progress through more rooms of the house, and examine deeper relationships, you will see that you don't let everybody into your bedroom, which is reserved for tried and true intimacy. One of the problems with people in churches is that they let too many people into the intimate areas of their life. Wisdom would say, move slowly and be wise.

****I am not implying that Elijah or Elias or David or Samuel or any of the people that I reference in this book followed this particular pattern."*

Chapter 2

The Formal Area

RELATIONSHIPS

Relationships will either advance the Kingdom of God or adversely limit our Kingdom potential. Perhaps you have been limited by negative relationships and how they affected you. You are not as effective in the Kingdom of God, because you have been hurt in a relationship and because of the pain that you carry. It is important that we see how relationships can impact us either positively or negatively, and how much God wants to fulfill in us through connecting in relationships.

Relationships take on different meanings or different levels which requires different boundaries. Anybody who is wise in God knows what kind of boundaries to set and how to set them. If you've ever made mistakes in relationships, you probably realized that you did not set the right kind of boundaries. If you would have set the right ones, the pain level would have been considerably diminished.

The Word of God says that our bodies are the temple of the Holy Spirit. The Old Testament temple or Tabernacle of God can be perceived as an analogy for relationships. The Tabernacle was portable but had a specific design and purpose. It was divided into three main parts; the outer court, the inner court, and the Holy of Holies. The "outer court" was larger than the "inner court" and the "inner court" was larger than the "Holy of Holies." You had to enter through the outer court following the prescribed process for access. At that time, only the ceremonial clean priest could enter the Holy of Holies which was the place to receive forgiveness of sin. If the priest was not ceremonially cleansed, he would die when he entered the Holy of Holies, which represented access to the Holy presence of God. At that particular time (before

> *If you are not in a good relationship with God, your ability to discern spiritual things will be drastically skewed.*

Christ), sin could not stand up in God's Presence. If they were unclean, they would immediately drop dead in the Holy Presence of God. You will notice that not everyone who entered the outer court made it to the inner court and only the priest could access God. There are people in your life whom God intended to remain in the "outer court" of your life or the "formal area."

Of course, since we live in New Testament, we have access to God through the redemptive work of Christ. In other words, Christ died so that we could enter the presence of God and furthermore receive, not death, but the grace and forgiveness of God. However, we cannot benefit from the "Holy" presence of God unless we walk in His forgiveness. God will always love us, but He cannot bless us if we are not repentant. Our ability to access the fullness of the presence of God is determined by our ability to walk in His cleansing power.

Earlier, I wrote about Front Porch relationships with people who remain on the front porch of our life and not allowed access until the relationship can be tested. The relationship is continually being tested so that a person can stay on the front porch for an indeterminate amount of time and only you can determine when they become closer to your life. As I have already stated, it is critical is that you use the right kind of discernment, that which flows out of your pure relationship with God, in relationships so that you know what to allow and disallow. If you are not in a good relationship with God, your ability to discern spiritual things will be drastically skewed. It will leave you more confused because your decisions are based more and feeling than Godly wisdom.

The Formal Area

I am going to use the term "Formal Area" to mean either the formal living room or the formal dining room. Most new homes do not even have formal living rooms however, growing up we had a formal living room that basically we never used. It had the nicest furniture and nice carpet and fixtures, but it was reserved for guests only. We couldn't go into the formal living room for fear that something would get messed up. I am glad they started building houses without formal living rooms because I could never figure out why you would have such a big room, make such a big deal over it and then hardly ever use it.

WHO'S IN YOUR HOUSE?

When the formal living room was used to entertain guests, it was typically the "surface" type of conversations, either one-sided where someone was coming for spiritual counsel or it was for "light" conversation. The picture I have in my mind is this is where you sit properly, never slouching, and sip your drink while holding your little pinky in the air. Sounds a bit stuffy but by the nature of the way the room was set up, it was intended for formal use only.

The formal dining room was to entertain guests but, in our family, it was also a way to get all the kids quiet for dinner. My mother would set the dining room table with the fine china, candles, and a nice southern cooked dinner. The rule in our house was when we had a dinner like that, we had to whisper. Talking loudly was not allowed and we were certainly not allowed to argue, which we typically did at dinner time. As I got older, I realized how wise my mother was to plan such a dinner just to have a peaceful, quiet evening together as family. Since there were two adults (Mom and Dad), and four children, it was known to get rowdy at the kitchen. You should try my Mom's little secret sometime, instead of sitting around the table and eating on paper plates, you ought to get the china out and have a nice dinner with the family, light some candles and tell everyone to act civil and use your "inside voice" and have a calm, peaceful family meal. Remember the rules!

As we move forward, we will refer to these two areas; the Formal Living Room and the Formal Dining Room as The Formal area. One of the really great things about the Formal Area is that if you invite someone new in, and after testing the relationship, you see that there are hidden agendas, it is so much easier to make corrections. You can thank them for the "wonderful" time together, subtly end the evening, and send them on their way. It is easier to re-evaluate and change there, than it is if they had been allowed into more intimate areas of your life. They were invited by you, and typically want to impress you and follow your house rules, but sometimes, with the greatest of intentions, that doesn't work. Their true colors come out.

Remember, this is important because the biggest mistake that most people make is getting too close too fast. I believe in these "Holy hook-ups," where God will put you together by the Spirit. But only select, God ordained, relationships are designed for that and they require discernment as well. They are in the formal area for a reason…to be tested.

This is true in any relationships within the Body of Christ. When you get too close too fast, you get hurt just as fast, and the closer they are, the greater the pain you will experience. When you get hurt in an intimate relationship, it is much more damaging. This is an example of why most people say that divorce in marriage carries the same weight of grieving that takes place in the death of a loved one. It is like a death because of the intimacy you once shared with that person, and now you suffer the loss of that intimate connection.

Your husband or your wife should be your best friend. You should not have a friend who is closer than your own spouse. If that person, being the very closest, most intimate friend in your life, said something critical or hurt you in some way, that would hurt you more than it would if someone else, like a front porch person or a formal person, hurt you. If pain comes from somebody who knows you that well, it hurts more. This should also remind spouses to be careful what you say to each other because intimacy has allowed your words to carry a lot of weight and impact. Furthermore, it is hard, if not almost impossible, to take back.

What we want are Kingdom relationships. We need to understand how to draw the right kind of boundaries and to effectively discern, manage, and maintain control from a Godly, balanced perspective. I have been in the ministry for many years and there are times where I have wanted to ask God to let me have about 15 totally selfish minutes so that I could let somebody have what, my emotional self, thinks "they deserve." Those are the kinds of rants that get us in trouble. We would much rather be Christ-like, knowing that it will produce a much more positive result. If you understand the necessity of drawing boundaries and drawing the right kind of boundaries from the beginning, the damage will be minimal.

Hurting People Hurt People

Early on in my years of ministry, there were times that I would say, "God, just give me something else to do, because there's too much hurt and pain from these crazy relationships in ministry." If you think that way, your ministry already has been negatively impacted. Perhaps it has already altered how you treat people or how you have disconnected from the true, Godly, relationship process. There is a lot of hurt and pain but there is also a Kingdom promise, the power of God to overcome in all situations, and the ability, to walk in wisdom. As the Proverb says, *"Wisdom is the principle thing, therefore, get wisdom."*

Many people leave churches and their God-given purpose because Christians hurt other Christians. Pastors are not exempt, they hurt people, people hurt pastors, and the cycle repeats. Churches tend to implode when that happens because pain is cyclical and will carry on through the church, stunting the Kingdom growth that God intended. If allowed to continue without breaking the cycle, the church implodes. It cannot be affective outside the four walls because of weakness. A church that truly loves and unites together and portrays a true, Godly example of family to the world, is a church that is unlimited on its impact on the world.

Maybe you have seen videos of buildings being imploded. Before they could build Phillips Arena in Atlanta, they had to first tear down the Omni Arena. When they imploded the Omni, the outside of the building looked to be intact, then the inside began to crumble, and the outside crumbled in on top. It goes the same with churches; when the process of hurting people first begins, internally explosives are going off and nobody seems to know what to do. Things can even look Spiritual, they look like good churches on the surface, but they implode because they are being very critical of others, and there is the absence of genuine love, and the presence of way too much unresolved pain. Someone once said, "the church is the only army that shoots its own wounded." This is so true with some churches.

It is by hurting people that the Body of Christ becomes seriously diseased and sick. We should never be about hurting other people, for any reason. Our focus should always be on healing and on God's presence manifesting in us, through us, and around us. The Word of God says we are supposed to love everybody. As much as that is true, it doesn't mean that we are supposed to invite everybody into our home and certainly not into the intimate areas of our life. In other words, He says we are to love them, not let them move in with us…that is, of course unless He specifically tells you to do that in an isolated situation.

> **It's your responsibility to discern what God allows through the exercise of wisdom.**

You cannot have dozens of people in your intimate life, you will never succeed. All friends are not intimate friends. I believe that your spouse should be your best friend and, at the most, you may have one or two other people in the intimate area. But you should always keep your spouse on the top of the list. If your spouse is not your best friend, and your work buddy is your best friend, you need to change friends. Furthermore, never allow someone of the opposite sex to be an intimate friend. That's not wisdom and it's not God!

Levels

It is important to understand these boundaries and how important they are for relationships to be healthy and vibrant. Earlier, I said that a front porch friend is still a "friend." Friends can enjoy all that the friendship will allow and find great fulfillment personally and spiritually. But don't go around asking people where you are in their lives, "Am I on the front porch of your life?" Don't ask them. If they ask you, don't answer. It's your responsibility to discern what God allows through the exercise of wisdom. As far as they are concerned, it's irrelevant.

People will not like the idea of being on the front porch, where they want to be in the bedroom. Usually, they have impure motives and are seeking to gain access to your life for the purpose of control or some other selfish agenda. They may be in denial but they have that kind of motive, which is why you must figure it to maintain your God-given identity. They do not deserve to be in the bedroom and should remain on the front porch. Remember, there is nothing wrong with the front porch and they are still your friend.

There is nothing wrong with the formal area. It's part of who you are and part of God's design for you. Would you appreciate an invitation from The President to fly to the White House and spend time with him in the formal living room of the White House? Would you leave the White House, after having spent time with the President, get on the plane home, and be mad because he did not invite you into the kitchen? Or would you just appreciate having been in the living room of the White House? After spending time with the President, would you be angry because he didn't call you on your birthday or invite you over for Christmas dinner? Hopefully, you are more balanced than that. However, you would tell everyone that you spent time with the President of the United States.

There is nothing wrong with being in the "formal area" in relationships. Kingdom things can happen from this type of relationship. Some relationships start out good and turn bad. Some start out bad and turn good. Some start out good, turn bad, and become good again. So, when we look at different types of friends, not all friends are supposed to be intimate friends. Relationships must continually be tested for you to decide what that relationship is supposed to be. Please note that it is better to distance yourself from someone who has not been allowed in to closely in the first place, than to have to disconnect from someone you have allowed yourself to become too close.

Testing

Have you ever had somebody come into your life and you knew they had a bad agenda? Motives must be pure and they must be tested. Elijah tested Elisha three times. Jesus tested the disciples. Jesus said, *"If you're going to come after me, you must deny yourself and take up the cross and follow me."* He tested them in their relationships. Some relationships were intended to go beneath the surface, but some were intended to stay right where they are. Do not think that intimacy is the ultimate answer or goal. Relationships that become intimate must start out as formal first. That is why two people make a serious mistake when they allow sexual intimacy before marriage. Because they have not yet had the time to really "know" each other and test the relationship before marriage and intimacy. It leads to the lack of respect for each other. That is what happens in churches when there are inappropriate socially intimate relationships…there is no mutual respect. It would be a tragedy if you began your relationship with Christ as intimate before you feared and revered Him. Intimacy grows out of the ongoing development of your walk with God. The more you spend time with Him, the more you know Him. The more you know Him, the more time you spend with Him. That dynamic equals intimacy!

I have tried to express this to people: God is not your "buddy," God is your friend. When there is that kind of disrespect and irreverence for God, nothing Kingdom comes out of our relationship with Him. God just becomes your "buddy" or pal. If someone asks you, "Who's that you're living for?" You say, "Oh, that's just God. He's my buddy." That implies that God can be moved simply by relationship and not by respectful reverence. Instead, you should say, "That is God, my Strong Friend, and my Redeemer." You need to fear Him, respect Him, reverence Him, and then understand Him as a friend. He can never be your friend until you understand how to respect Him. The same is true of all relationships. You cannot become close to somebody until they first respect you and what you stand for.

We never want to purposely allow anyone in our life who knowingly is going to hurt us. You "love" them, but you don't allow the unnecessary influence of their imbalance to corrupt your path or slow down you progress.

But remember, just because somebody has been tested and possibly even pushed out because they have revealed something impure or gone through bad behavior, does not mean that they cannot come back. Paul had to distance himself from John Mark, but later was moved to invite him back into his life for a Kingdom purpose. Relationships are always being put to the test. Don't put somebody out of your life and divorce yourself from them forever. At the same time, don't allow them to take advantage of you, because they may have a hidden agenda.

Can you see the foundation? Relationships are very powerful and a lot of good can flow out of healthy, Godly, relationships. It is said that you are just four people away from the President of the United States. That means you know someone, who knows someone, who knows someone, who knows someone, who knows the President of the United States. Can you imagine that? God connects people and puts them into relationships for a reason. Do not underestimate what God can do. But a relationship should never be about you or personal gain. They are always about the Kingdom and what God can do through them. As my life becomes more seasoned and my walk with God more intimate, I am all about the Kingdom God and how relationships are a vital part of God's plan. I cherish the relationships that God allows me to have. Many times, I tell God how thankful I am that He has allowed me to be connected to certain people that I have so much respect for.

The Tapestry

Ephesians 2:10 says, *"For we are God's workmanship created in Christ Jesus to do good work."* Think about that. Can you envision that you are God's workmanship? He didn't make a mistake when He made you. You are a multi-billion-dollar individual. Praise God! You have value. Do you know why? Because you are an original, not a copy. You are the handiwork of God, He spoke you into existence. You are not a fake, you're an original. *"...Which God prepared in advance for us to do those good works."* Paul likens God to a sculpture who fashions each one of us uniquely, and in doing so, has a specific plan and purpose for our lives. What an awesome thing! You cannot be somebody else. You can only be who you are in Christ.

One of the biggest mistakes that you could make would be to act like somebody else-imitate how they walk, how they talk, how they preach, how they sing. You need to be you, because God fashioned you for His purpose and has given you everything you need to fulfill that purpose. I often say, "God doesn't call the equipped, he equips the called."

If you look at the front of a tapestry, you will see a specific design or a picture. But if you turn the tapestry over, there will be knots and pieces of string hanging out. It is difficult to discern what the picture really is if you are looking at it from the back. God deals with all the knots, all the twine, all the excess, all the difficulties in your life—He sees the finished product on the other side. In God's eyes, you are a completed work. He knows where He is going with you, and if you allow Him to work in you, you will see the unique handiwork of God.

Some of you are living all confused and botched up because you are trying to look at the back side of the tapestry. God does not make mistakes with your life. God did not use the wrong thread, make the wrong turn, or wrong stitch–God is creating a masterpiece in you. You have to see the finished product is beautiful and complete and allow God to fulfill what He wants in you. Try it without God and you will have a mess. If you let God do it, it will be a masterpiece.

Pleasant Formality

Now, when you let people into the formal living area of your life, the relationship remains on a formal level. You are still friends, but you are mindful of where the relationship is.

One time, I was invited to a prominent member of the community's house for dinner. Prior to the dinner, I only knew the husband of this couple as a rigid, no frills, no fun type of person. The first thing I thought was, "This is going to be a boring, stiff, formal evening," because I knew we were going to sit in the formal dining room and everything was going to be proper, and I just wasn't really looking forward to that kind of evening out. We certainly would not be kicking off our shoes, or propping our feet up to have a good time. I arrived at their house, and sure enough, I walked into the foyer (they had nice imported rugs all over the house, and expensive, extravagant furniture) and looked over in the dining room. It was all set up for the evening meal, there were multiple forks, knives, and spoons. Each place setting had two drink glasses. What am I supposed to do with all this stuff? Who's going to clean all these dishes? Isn't this a little too much?

His wife invited us to be seated at the table. We pulled ourselves up to those hard, throne like, dining room chairs. It was not very long into our dinner when the host began to tell jokes. He told a joke that reminded me of a joke that reminded him of a joke, and it went on and on. About four hours later, we were still sitting at the same table with all the leftover food around us, having the best time.

Formal relationships do not have to be stiff. You can party-and I mean Christian party-in a formal relationship. You can have a blast in a formal relationship. I walked out of that house saying, "Those people are awesome." I did not walk out saying, "Well they didn't take me into the kitchen, so I'm offended." I walked out saying, "They were fun. We had a good time. I like them. They are wonderful people."

A Biblical Example

It is time to talk about Elijah and Elisha and their relationship because there is a dynamic that comes from this kind of a relationship. Both men were prophets in Israel and had the prophetic call of God on their lives. Miracles were flowing out of their lives. But, there were differences. Elijah had a poor background and did not come from a wealthy family. Elisha came from Abel Maholah and the Scripture says that he had 12 oxen which was a sign of wealth.

You cannot just pick people who are "like" you for relationship. Just because somebody is not like you, doesn't mean that you should have nothing to do with them. Their weaknesses may be your strengths and your weaknesses may be their strengths. God will bring the two of you together and His Kingdom work will be accomplished by what you become together.

Elijah and Elisha had differences and God used them. God will also you use you if there are differences in your relationships. Elijah had some issues and mood swings. He went from euphoria to depression; he was either doing really well or he was doing really badly. Elisha seemed to be a little more even tempered. Elijah was described as hairy. Elisha obviously was bald. So that means long haired people can hang out with short haired people. Elisha's ministry lasted twice as long as Elijah's. Elisha's ministry had twice as many miracles as Elijah's, hence the double portion of Elijah's spirit on Elisha. Twice as much came out of his life because he asked for a double portion of Elijah's spirit. If you compare miracles you will see that they are different, yet they're all miracles. There were differences in their lives, but there was a dynamic that existed in that relationship. You will find people with different abilities and different gifts. You must recognize that God might be putting them in your life so that He can bring together all the parts of the body to accomplish His work.

Consider the relationship between a picture and its frame. A good frame draws attention to the picture. If the frame takes the attention away from the picture, then the frame is not fulfilling its purpose. In the body of Christ, we are the frame and God is the picture. If we take the emphasis away from the picture, and put its emphasis on us, then in essence, we are saying, "I want to be the picture, God. You be the frame." God must be first, we must be second. John said, "That I would decrease so that Christ might increase." You do not want to be the picture. You just want to be the frame. And you want to let God fashion your life so that you are drawing attention to the picture.

Pointers

Let's examine the dynamics of a formal relationship.

1. *Formal relationships are a perfect testing ground*. You allow a person into your house and your life, but you are still guarded, still formal. You are going to test to discern God's will for it. Elijah tested Elisha three times, but Elisha hung on. He called Elijah his father and hung on to him. This could have been very frustrating for Elisha. Sometimes we get very frustrated with the quirks of the other person and we leave. Being frustrated is not an excuse to leave or disconnect from a relationship. Elisha wanted Elijah's anointing. He said, "I want a double portion of

Elijah's spirit." The testing nature of a Formal relationship leads to the second point.

2.   *Formal relationships remain guarded, so you can see if there are any hidden agendas.* Ask yourself, "Does this person like me for selfish reasons?" In Formal relationships, your position is important. Young ladies, how you position yourself in a relationship with a man will determine how quickly that man gets into your life. When you position yourself, you remain guarded because you are looking for agendas. Does a person want you for something that is wrong when they should want you because they trust, respect, and reverence you? Does this person want something for their own selfish gain? I discover this in ministry all the time. Often, people will seek a relationship with me because they want to be a minister. If I find out that is all they want,

then I distance myself, because I do not want people who want to use me just as a portal to a position or role in the church. I remain open and loving, and, as far as they are concerned I'm still nice and friendly, but they will never get anywhere with me until they seek purity in their own life and lay their agendas down. I have seen people fail miserably, while getting upset with me that I'm not giving them a chance, and they move on and take their agenda to another church only to watch it play out the same way.

You always put relationships to the test. Will you be hurt? Yes. Will you make mistakes? Yes. But you have to dare to risk. So, in the place of testing, you must remain guarded. Some people are going to become jealous and obviously, jealousy is not healthy for a relationship. Impure motives do not make a healthy relationship. Defenses like that of Fort Knox, do not make a healthy relationship. There have been times when I have spoken to people that I might as well have been talking to a brick wall. I just want to say, "I wish you would tear that wall down long enough for me to just see what you are really like." People can become so guarded that it is difficult for Kingdom agendas to flow out of their relationships.

3. *Formal relationships become a good pivot position.* Many of you may not understand the physics behind pivoting, but if you watch basketball, you will see that a pivot man is essential. The pivot man is typically called the center because the pivot point is at the middle and has the liberty to go anywhere. When you pivot, you can go here, go there, back up, or go forward. In the same way, a formal relationship is the perfect pivot position. It can go either direction. It is still safe. It is better for you to say, "You know what? It's really been nice. I'll see you

later." when you're in the formal area, then it is when they're in the den with their shoes off, wearing their pajamas, with a popcorn bucket in their laps. At that point it is a lot more difficult to say, "You know what? You need to get out of my house." There is a big difference.

We used to have prayer at the church every morning at 6 am, seven days a week. It was a handful of men that would join with us for one hour of personal prayer time. We would occasionally have someone decide to join us during this time. One morning a man, I'll call him George (not his real name), who had been in the church for about a year, started coming and praying with us at six. He drove a good distance from his house to pray with us and it was not really on his way to work, so he had to backtrack a little to head into Atlanta each morning. After a while, he realized that it was just going to be him and me and maybe one or two other people at the church for prayer. So one morning George said to me, "I have been thinking about this and I think it would be better if you came to my house and we prayed at my house at 6 every morning instead of coming to the church." I 'looked at him and said, "I'm not comfortable coming to your house at 6 to pray in your living room while your wife is asleep in the bedroom adjacent to your living room. Sorry, but I'm not willing to do that." He became angry with me. So, I said to him, "Why do you want to do that?" He said, "Because it's too far for me to drive."

Now, if I had been more focused on pleasing man than doing what was right, I might have given in to his request, just so he wouldn't reject me, and God forbid, possibly leave the church. Now I know that some of you are much stronger than this and you would have any problem standing up for what you know to be right. However, I'm sharing this because many of you are "people-pleasers" and, many times you compromise your convictions for the sake of acceptance from your peers.

This is one of the biggest mistakes that people can make. Never allow yourself to compromise in something just for the purpose of being accepted. It's like inviting a bad spirit into your house because you want somebody to like you. If you are going to do drugs, run around with them, or drink just so they will like you, it's like inviting a known thief to move into your home just because you want his acceptance. Call things what they are and stand up for what is right, regardless of potential consequences.

4.   *Formal relationships are a good place for introspection.* This is a good place to take some time to look at yourself. Have you built impenetrable

walls around your life emotionally? Do you have impure motives? Do you have impure agendas? If you do, you need to deal with them before you have healthy, vibrant relationships. Introspection is good because you have invited somebody in and now you have a friend in the formal area of your life-this is a good place for you evaluate yourself.

5.   *Formal relationships keep you from becoming a Spiritual orphan.* If you have built walls around you like Fort Knox, then you have probably constructed a fortress of unnecessary protection that has you imprisoned alone, with little hope of ever experiencing the beauty of a God-style of connectedness. You build walls so that people cannot get in, but eventually you find out that those same walls are keeping you from getting out. You've become a Spiritual orphan and an unproductive

WHO'S IN YOUR HOUSE?

Christian, because God intended for you to have relationships for His Kingdom purpose in your life. Being a Spiritual orphan is like being stranded all alone on an island. You feel completely alone in this big world of activity and relationships.

When I was little, I watched movies where people were stranded on islands. They would usually end up doing strange things because they did not interact with other people. Sometimes, I think people unknowingly orchestrate this, so they don't have to deal with the pain that comes from normal human interaction. It's an attempt to build something that will not endure the tests and surprises of life. You start to build a world around you, instead of trying to be the person God created you to be, to walk in His wisdom, and experience the beauty of connectedness.

6.   *The formal area is where people should see the best in you.* Some might say, "But, you should just be open and transparent all the time." Does that mean it would be alright for me to walk up to someone and say, "Hello, my name is Fritz, and I have a problem with depression and anxiety. In fact, I have all kinds of issues. I'm struggling with losing my joy and peace. I'm having financial problems and I'm just so depressed and discouraged. By the way, it's nice to meet you."

I don't do that. You don't do that! You do everything to present your best self. You stay positive, standing in faith that you're going to make it, and God is in control! This doesn't deny that you have problems. It just doesn't allow those problems to be the thing that defines who you are. In the formal area, people don't need to know every fault, shortcoming, and detail of your life. They don't need to know because they can take all of that personal information and use it against you. You need to be cautious and wise about discussing your problems with too many people.

This doesn't mean that you should be skeptical or cynical of everybody. It simply means you just need to sharpen your discernment skills. If you have been hurt before, one of the ways to avoid it in the future is to ask God to give you the ability to discern a situation for you to allow that relationship to survive the test of time and your control on what you allow, and when you allow it. Say to yourself, "I will walk in the wisdom of God and dare to risk but not be played as a fool or a pushover by the dominance or manipulation of others. I am not going to invite someone into the intimate areas of my life, knowing that their heart is not pure."

Please understand if you risk it and someone does take advantage of you, allow God to give you the grace to be strong and to protect you from harm. He will give you the grace to keep moving forward in Him. You will also be wiser from your experience. When random experiences are not the norm, it's much easier to deal with.

7. *A formal relationship can lead to a strong mentoring relationship.* Good leadership always starts with a formal relationship. It is when you lose a sense of reverence and awe of God that you start to tell God what He needs to do for you instead of listening to what you need to do in Him. A relationship with God begins with reverence, respect. fear, and awe of His presence. This puts you on a path of true intimacy with Him, knowing that you would never do anything to take advantage of who He is in your life.

WHO'S IN YOUR HOUSE?

God is not Santa Claus, the ice cream man, or the candy man. He is God. He is to be feared and respected. He's not standing there with a big stick ready to beat you. He loves you. He desires that closeness and intimacy with you. But we must respect and honor Him first. Likewise, in mentoring relationships, there must be respect for the mentor before the mentor can truly impact your life. If you lose respect for someone, you can no longer learn anything from them.

Elisha washed the hands of Elijah. When the student takes advantage of the mentoring relationship, he is no longer able to be mentored. As soon as he thinks you're his friend and not his mentor/leader, he begins to think he can get away with taking advantage of you. When this happens, he loses the ability to respect what the mentor can do. Spiritual parenting flows best when there is a foundation of respect. If you want a Spiritual father, you need to respect that Spiritual father, and honor his "fatherly" leadership. If you have a Spiritual mother, you need to respect that Spiritual mother in the same way. We need more Spiritual parental figures in the church.

Coming Together

In I Timothy, Paul said to Timothy, *"To Timothy, my true son in the faith, grace, mercy and peace from God the Father and Christ Jesus our Lord."* Ruth and Naomi, even though they had a mother in-law, daughter in-law relationship, they had mutual respect. Paul and Timothy had mutual respect for each another. There was mutual respect with Christ and the disciples. Christ said, *"Deny yourself, take up the cross, follow me. Go sell everything you*

have. Let's go. Give your business to somebody else
and follow me." Even when Christ spoke certain
things into their lives, the disciples had respect for
Him. Elijah and Elisha had respect for each other.

Elisha says to Elijah, *"My father, my father"*
because he respected Elijah. In 1 Kings 19:16, the
Lord instructs Elijah to anoint Elisha, who is supposed
to take his place as a prophet in Israel. All these
relationships existed to bring about God's Kingdom
purpose. Elijah was not there to be Elisha's buddy. He
was there to anoint Elisha to be a prophet and
prepare him for the God's purpose. Paul said to
Timothy in II Timothy 1:6, *"For this reason I remind*
you to fan into flame the gift of God, which is in you
through the laying on of hands." What he's saying to
Timothy is, *"I laid hands on you. Be encouraged. Fan*
the flame. You got it going on man! You can do this!
Get to it!"

Paul is speaking encouragement and blessing into his life. He is encouraging his Spiritual son to remember that he laid his hands on him to bless him for God's purpose. This should be happening more in the church. We should be fanning the flame of the gift of God in people and encouraging them to walk out God's special plan and purpose for them.

Our relationship with God has been tested. There is a calling on our lives and an anointing for God's power to be revealed. When you focus on being discouraged,

> *You are uniquely fashioned by God. God has His purpose woven through the tapestry of your life. He is the picture, you and I are the frame.*

depressed, or dejected and rejected, then you can't see that God has a powerful call on your life to experience His greatness. Remember, you are more than a conqueror! Fan into flame that gift from God! The enemy wants you to doubt your calling or think that you aren't sharp enough to succeed. He will do whatever he can to convince you to stand at the front door of your relationships and keep everybody you know on the front porch of your life.

Do you think the enemy is pleased with that? You better believe it. The call of God is on your life. You are uniquely fashioned by God. God has His purpose woven through the tapestry of your life. He is the picture, you and I are the frame. He's been with you through thick and thin, good and bad. Understanding the magnitude of what God can do with relationships, will bring you to a deeper understanding of how to operate in His Kingdom's purpose. Remember, it's ultimately about each of us living out the purpose of the Divine Creator.

Chapter 3
THE KITCHEN

BASICS

If we do not understand this concept of relationships, we're going to be much less effective for God. Many Christians are not living at the level they should, because they have dysfunctional relationships. They have problems, pain, and hurt that has come out of past relationships. You might have been in a relationship with someone who hurt you, and you decided to draw your own emotional conclusions and make certain decisions for your life.

I can tell you, that in most cases, if you make decisions based on what you feel you're going to make the wrong decision. For example, you might say, "I'll never a trust a man again. I'll never a trust a woman again. I'll never trust a pastor again." These bold, broad sweeping statements will ultimately have a negative impact in your life. There are people that have existed for years being held back from God's best because they have decided that they will "never be hurt again", so they decide to be 100% guarded and never allow themselves to be vulnerable.

You need to understand the magnitude of God's desire to fulfill his Kingdom purpose through the relationships that He allows along the way. Certain people belong on the front porch of your life, thus giving you the opportunity to test that relationship. You must be the one to set the boundaries. Part of the problem with most people is that they have allowed others into their lives too fast which means the relationship won't be properly tested. The quicker and the closer you allow them in, the more pain it will cause you if you get hurt. So, to ensure that there's the least amount of pain, you need

Godly wisdom to determine the boundaries. You need to be thinking about how God will allow all kinds of relationships for you and seeking His advice on how to exercise Godly wisdom to handle those relationships.

Just because somebody wants to be your close friend, doesn't mean that they have a right to be. I used to be a little bit like my dad in the sense that whenever the phone would ring, I would drop everything to answer the phone. But I heard Mike Murdoch make a statement one time, "Just because you're calling me means you want to talk to me, but it doesn't mean I want to talk to you."

That may sound a little harsh, but I'm trying to illustrate point. Many times, we will move heaven and earth just because somebody wants us to like them. Just because they want to come into our lives, we allow them in, and the quicker we allow them in, the more damage can do in the relationship, and the more pain it brings to you.

God's Purpose

It's important to know that God's grace is enough to heal you of any pain that you have gone through or will go through in relationships. The worst thing that you could do is decide not to ever allow anyone into your life again.

But you must be wise in relationships. Imagine allowing someone into your house with several young children, and the kids were climbing on the furniture and the walls, and you are thinking, "I can't way until they get out of my house because they're going to tear everything up." You allowed them in and they created problems for you that required a desire for their removal. Has someone come into your house and caused havoc? As a Christian, you are going to stand by your own moral and ethical standards, so now you start looking for a way to get them out of your house. You take a strong stance on what you will allow or disallow.

We don't allow certain movies to be viewed in our home. We have a "house standard." Your house standard may be different from ours and that's okay. But, the important thing is that you set the standard in your house and you enforce it if someone chooses to go against it.

It should be the same for relationships. When you test a relationship, you allow them into your life, you are responsible for setting and maintaining what you will allow or not allow. God intended for you to have relationships, but He never intended for all of them to be your best friend.

Discernment

I keep reiterating that you need to be wise in relationships. Keep asking God for wisdom and discernment. I've been in ministry for more than 30 years and I was not that wise in the beginning. I allowed myself to be too vulnerable. It's critical that you not make bad decisions based on bad experiences, or emotional decisions out of deep emotional hurt. It's imperative that you understand your mistakes so that you can be wiser, learning more with each step. Let's examine II John 7-11, *"Many deceivers who do not acknowledge Jesus Christ as coming in the flesh have gone out into the world, any such person is the deceiver and the anti-Christ. Watch out that you do not lose what you have worked for but that you may be rewarded fully."*

I frequently say that "for every new level, there's a new devil." Have you ever noticed that when you get to a certain level in life, somebody will come into your life to agitate you and irritate the whole process? I'm talking about well-meaning people; those that love you, they love God, and they're thinking right but they're not doing right. They're the ones that are in the wrong, but it's messing up your progress. They will end up setting you back a little from what God is trying to fulfill in you unless you decide that you're going to set the right kind of boundaries in relationships.

In verse 9-11, John says, *"Anyone who runs ahead and does not continue in the teaching of Christ does not have God. Whoever continues in the teaching has both the Father and the Son. If anyone comes to you and does not bring this teaching do not take him into your house or welcome him. Anyone who welcomes him shares in his wicked work."*

WHO'S IN YOUR HOUSE?

Now I need to make a disclaimer; I am not suggesting that Christians should not fellowship with non-Christians. This is not about exclusivity. However, you want

> *We need to watch ourselves and monitor our own strengths and weaknesses, and keep our feet planted in God.*

to be careful about allowing a weaker person in your life. Your vision must be clear on why what the overall purpose is of that relationship, and it should be for winning them to Christ or mentoring them out of their struggle. If all you do is hang out with nonbelievers, you will become more like them in your thinking and behavior. We cannot be exclusive because we are supposed to be with the world to win the world. However, like Jesus, we're in the world, but we're not of the world. We're supposed to make an impact on the world, but we can't impact them for God if we're weak and struggle.

If the world is changing you and you are not changing the world, you need to get closer to God and become stronger in Him before you decide to hang out with weaker people. Stay more with God before you do anything in the world. Some people transform into the world within minutes of being around worldly things. Their speech changes, and their decision-making ability becomes skewed. Before you know it, they have taken on the nature of worldly things. We are called to live Godly lives. We need to watch ourselves and monitor our own strengths and weaknesses, and keep our feet planted in God.

Necessary Confrontation

We have talked about the necessity of confronting in relationships at every level because everyone understands what it's like to have a Judas in your camp. They tell you that you are the greatest and they have your back! They think you're the best person they've ever met. They laugh at your jokes and love your stories. Whenever I hear this from someone, I immediately observe them for a season. Sometimes I will even "test" them to see how loyal they are. The next thing you know they're easily offended and turning on you. When this happens, you just went from Hero to Zero in one swoop. What do you have to do? You have to confront it.

If you have a Spirit on you that doesn't like to be rejected, you need to get delivered from it. People that have the Spirit-of-not-wanting-to-be-rejected-by-people will stand there, tolerate, and allow all kind of foolishness just because they want to be loved and don't want to be rejected. They will allow things into their lives that are damaging and will bring ultimate destruction if they don't confront it.

Listen, if it's not God and it's not consistent with the character of God, get on it immediately. Deal with it, confront it, and get it out of your house. Now when you kick somebody out of your emotional house, you're not kicking them out forever. You still "love" them and the grace of God is still there, but you have established new boundaries. You're not saying, *"Depart from me."* You are saying, *"You're not going to be this close anymore."* This step is huge, so remember, you are the one in control when it comes to people running their own agendas that are contrary to your overall growth and productivity.

Memories Around The Kitchen Table

I was raised in the South, and in the South everybody sat around the kitchen table for hours and tell jokes and stories. Sometimes we would stay up until 2 or 3 in the morning, drinking coffee, eating dessert, and just having a good time. That is something very familiar for me, and it's a great memory from growing up.

When I was younger, we had some friends who traveled in their own custom bus, singing gospel music. One night some friends of ours who traveled from Florida pulled their bus into our front yard around 1 a.m., and start blowing the horn, shining their headlights on our front door. Obviously, we were all asleep and awakened by this excessive noise. We turned on the light, got out of bed and went downstairs and there was a big Greyhound bus staring at our front door. We knew who it was, so we all went outside. They got out of the bus, came in our house, and we sat around the kitchen table laughing and telling stories until the sun came up. That was a very fun time.

For me, the kitchen was a good place to relax a little bit and enjoy life. In this analogy, the kitchen is the casual, more relaxed part of a relationship. The kitchen is where the breakfast table is, where you sit and relax, drink coffee or tea and enjoy others. In some cases, you sit around the table, you laugh a little, and you tell stories.

If somebody came into your kitchen, sat down at your kitchen table, and the first thing they said was, "Your kitchen sure is ugly. I really don't like the cabinets. The floors don't look very clean. Somebody needs to clean it up around here. You have crumbs from your toaster that look like they've been there for a week and a half. Your refrigerator is all junked up. Somebody needs to clean that mess." What would you do? You would say, "My, my, look at the time. I just realized that I need to be somewhere in 15 minutes. I'm going to have to ask you to leave so I can get my things together. Let me show you the front door." They proved that they have no place in your home because they set themselves up as judge and jury on how you do things in your house. They failed the test.

There's something about your house that requires mutual respect. That's why Christians cannot allow themselves to be condescending and judgmental towards others. One of the worst things Christians can do is to become arrogant and proud. I don't know what it is about people, but sometimes, it takes them way too long to recognize serious character flaws and make changes for personal development. Then, once they get delivered from it, even though it took them forever, they expect you to change overnight. Patience is not a virtue with them.

You cannot be condescending as a Christian because you must remember your struggles, and that you are still a work in progress. The memory of what God brought you through will help you be more gracious and accepting of other people.

Relationships have nothing to do with acceptance or love. You love and accept people, regardless of who they are and what they do. Only allow the people that aren't going to damage or harm you, or the vision that God has given you.

God Loves You

Understand God's purpose in relationship. God is not keeping you on the front porch. He has invited you into His bedroom. God has invited you into an intimate relationship. When God gives an invitation He doesn't back out, when you mess up God doesn't kick you back out on the front porch. In your relationship with God, you are the one that decides how close you will be. He won't be able to bless you and protect you like He wants to if you decide to do things your own way. A relationship with God is a privilege, but it's your choice.

I lived in a neighborhood one time, next to a new home that a couple had just purchased. The husband smoked cigarettes, and the wife didn't, so the wife decided to make a rule that there would be no smoking in the house. Anybody that wanted to smoke, including her husband, and all his friends, had to go outside. One day it was around 15 degrees outside, with the wind chill factor 20 or 30 degrees below 0. I looked out through our kitchen window and my neighbor was standing out on the back deck, shivering, smoking a cigarette. I thought to myself, well there's a rule in that house and he's abiding by it, if he's going to such measures to smoke outside.

This is so much like our relationship with God. We know there are certain things in our lives that dishonor God. By choosing to do those things, we have chosen to go back out to the front porch, and we distance ourselves from God by our choice of sin. Because the choice that we make is not consistent with the standard of God, we have exited the bedroom and gone to the front porch. We have disconnected from God. God never intended for this to happen, but it is by nature of our choices.

This is why, we must do everything to remain connected to God in relationship. A spousal relationship must be intimate in conversation and emotion. There must be a high level of respect, honor, and trust which fosters the highest levels of intimacy. It takes hard work and sacrifice to maintain intimacy.

A Healthy Family

Now let's go over the dynamics of the Kitchen, the casual relationship. Casual relationships are more like a true healthy family, where we all love and respect each other. If you don't have a healthy family, stop watching reality shows, and start following the Bible on how to love your family members in spite of how dysfunctional they are. Family is not about everyone being the same. It's about embracing our differences for the sake of loving each other. Family is not about cutting each other with caustic criticism or competing with one another.

When you allow somebody into your casual area of relationship and they're in competition with you, move them quickly to the front porch to maintain a formal relationship. If you allow somebody into your life and they're constantly criticizing everything, you need to start evaluating why you allow them to continue to cause harm to you and those around you.

> *There is still love, still grace, but this is a new level because these people have been tried and tested to be faithful for this level of relationship.*

In my family, I have a younger brother, a younger sister, and an older sister. Everyone is married, we all have children, and some have grandchildren, etc. We make it a habit to try to get together for Christmas and Thanksgiving, and we celebrate everyone's birthday in groups several times throughout the year. The one thing that we were taught growing up is that, no matter what our differences, we will love each other and be a healthy family unit. Obviously, this is almost impossible without God at the foundation. We have certainly had differences, but we have never allowed those differences to come between us.

WHO'S IN YOUR HOUSE?

The relationship should be like a healthy family because when you allow them into the kitchen, into the casual relationship, everybody's more vulnerable than they are in the formal dining room. In the formal dining room, everyone is keeping everything on the surface and less intimate. But in the kitchen, we're going to relax just a little bit, which makes us more vulnerable because we're more relaxed and trusting.

The conversation is different in the kitchen than in the formal area. We're still having fun, still friends, God's still using us, God's still in it. There is still love, still grace, but this is a new level because these people have been tried and tested to be faithful for this level of relationship. Beautiful things come out of these types of relationships because the level of trust is higher, so the expectations are higher.

You Are Like-Minded

In this casual-type relationship, people need to be more like-minded and spirited. In other words, you need to have the same vision about life. It's not going to make sense for someone to come into the casual area of your life and start talking about highly personal things. You want to be of like mind and spirit. Again, there's a mutual respect, but the Bible says in John 8:32, *"You'll know the truth and the truth will set you free."* In a casual-type relationship, doing the right thing is more important than somebody's opinion. Out of mutual respect, we keep our sharp opinions and feelings in check.

Transitioning in to better things

Casual relationships can transition from formal to intimate. There is always the potential of the relationship becoming more intimate as it is being tested. It's not a graduation from one to the other. Rather, it's a determination for where God wants the relationship to be based on the proper dynamics being in place. When the proper dynamics are in place, then that relationship was just approved by God for another level. Don't consider it a bad thing if most relationships remain front porch or formal. It's all part of God's plan. It's simply drawing proper, Godly boundaries.

Remember don't ever go up and ask somebody, "Where am I in your life? The kitchen? Am I on the front porch?" This is totally unnecessary and counter-productive. It's irrelevant to the other person where they are with you. The idea is that you determine your own personal and confidential boundaries.

We talked about the formal part being pivotal because you can adjust either way. You can still get to the front door. But in a casual relationship, it's more transitional towards another level of intimacy. The potential of pain is greater, simply because of the increased intimacy, but also because it's still a testing ground. It's just more difficult to get them out of your life the closer they get.

More Committed

Casual relationships are more committed. We need to be committed in giving to and serving one another. Some people in church are only in church because they can gain. These people are always receiving, and seldom give back. As we receive from the abundance of God, we should be more of a conduit for others. If we are in a committed relationship with God, then we are going to be more committed in relationships with others. Our relationship with God makes us more grounded in Him and His purpose for us. Psalm 40, verse 1-4 says, *"I waited patiently for the Lord. He turned to me and He heard my cry. He lifted me out of the slimy pit, out of the mud and mire. He set my feet on a rock. He gave me a firm place to stand. He put a new song in my mouth, a hymn of praise to our God. Many will see and fear and put their trust in the Lord. Blessed is the man. Blessed, happy, prosperous is the man who makes the Lord his trust and does not look to the proud, to those who turn aside to false God."*

Do you want to be blessed? The word "blessed" can be translated as happy, or prosperous. *"Blessed is the man who makes the Lord his trust."* Now let me ask you a question, is God committed to you? You know He is. So if God is committed to you, then you can be committed in relationships with others. There should be a higher level of commitment in a casual-type relationship. Personal relationships carry a high value and should be more precious than individual accomplishments.

Now let me further explain some of the dynamics of this house analogy. Not everybody in your family needs to be allowed past the kitchen area of your life. You love them, but they're a little strange or emotionally unstable. You thank God they don't have to live with you. They go to their house, you go to yours, and everybody gets a little break until we have an opportunity to be together again as family.

You still have to create boundaries and use discernment, even in your family. The same thing is true in the family of God. Not everybody in the family of God belongs in an intimate relationship with you. At the same time, they belong in your life and you have to respect who they are, along with what God is doing in their lives. Often in formal relationships people are receiving but they're not giving. Casual relationships are more give and take. If you allow someone into the kitchen (casual) area of your life, and all you do is give, it's going to wear you down.

I had a friend who bought a brand new luxury car. He and his wife were out of town, and a friend of theirs was flying into their city so they invited him to spend the night. My friend told the man where the key was, he said, *"Just go on in and enjoy the house. Spend the night. You don't have to pay for a hotel. We're out of and we will back in a couple of days. Just lock the house up when you leave."* When the homeowner called the next day, the phone rang but nobody answered. Then somebody was calling him from his own personal car phone. This friend had decided to take his car and drive two or three hundred miles around the state of Florida. Now we're talking about a pretty expensive luxury car. My friend said, *"Hey, what you doing?" He said, "Oh I'm out driving your car." He said, "You're doing what?" He said, "I'm driving your car. This is a nice car."* My friend was freaking out on the telephone, saying, *"Man, are you driving my car?" He said, "Yeah I've driven it. I've gone to Tampa and now I'm headed north and I'm just driving around. I have some errands to run. I hope you don't mind."*

I asked my friend what he did when he got home. He said, *"The first thing I did was check out my car."* He said, *"The second thing I did was to never leave my keys at the house ever again. And the third thing I did was to decide to never invite that man back into my house again. I didn't offer him the keys to the car. He took them because he's a taker and not a giver."*

Less Guarded

Casual relationships are less guarded. In Psalm 25, verse 14, it says, *"The LORD confides in those who fear him; he makes his covenant known to them."* .To confide in someone, they must be trusted. Have you ever gone to somebody and said, "Can you keep this a secret?" and they didn't keep it? Everyone has experienced this, and some have experienced it more than they are willing to confess. My dad jokingly says, "It's not me that can't keep a secret. It's the people I tell that can't keep them."

Casual relationships are less guarded because you should be able to trust whether you can confide in this person. Like every relationship, it must be tried and tested before you discuss personal and confidential things. All relationships have to be tested. Some people feel like they must answer when they are asked personal questions. There are some things that are not privy other people. Then you learn a pre-planned response, "that's really a personal/family matter and I would like to keep it that way." Wisdom says, "they don't need to know." No matter how much they ask, I'm not going to talk about it.

Trust Is Important

There has to be genuine trust. You cannot allow somebody in that you haven't built some level of trust with. If they borrowed your lawn mower, and haven't returned it for six months, you need to consider their trust level questionable. I talked to a Christian man who is very wealthy, people know he has money, and he has decided to never loan money. Do you know what he tells them when they ask to borrow money? He says, *"You're my friend and I want to keep it that way because when I give you money and you decide you can't pay me back I don't want you to feel bad."* Then they say, *"Oh I won't feel bad at all."* But he says, *"I want to keep you as a friend so I'm not going to loan you…"* I've heard him turn down people that were in desperate need in hopes that he would come through with a loan. Now, if he decides to give the money away, that is totally up to him. He is in complete control and able to do as the Holy Spirit leads him, without feeling pressured by their request. You have to come to the place where you can trust them not take advantage of you.

Risking is a necessary part of life

In casual relationships you have a greater risk of pain. The closer you allow them into your emotional house, when they hurt you, the more it will impact you emotionally. It's one thing to get hurt by somebody you don't know that well. It's another thing to get hurt by somebody you are close too. That's tough because when you open yourself up to somebody, and they abuse you, it's painful. It's so important that spouses realize how deep their words can cut when they are angry and say things that have lasting effects. You don't abuse each other with your words or actions, you should be highly selective. Many times people make drastic, emotional decisions when they are hurt by the close people in their lives.

There was a man that came to the church one Sunday. I met him at the back door and he said, *"Oh I love this church. It's great. Everybody's so loving and so giving and so caring and everything. This is great. I haven't been in a church in 15 years and I used to be an elder in a church."* I thought something was a little strange. He must have been hurt or offended. I said,

WHO'S IN YOUR HOUSE?

"Well why have you not been in church for 15 years?" He said, *"Oh it's a long story. The pastor at the church I went to really hurt me."* I said, *"Really?"* He said, *"Yeah the pastor hurt me so bad, that I've been angry and bitter for 15 years. Somebody told me about your church. I just decided to come today and I really like it. I think I'm going to get back in church."*

Of course, we loved him and welcomed him, even though he was saying more than he realized about what type of person he was, and where he could be in his relationship with God. I wanted to say to him, "I hope and pray that I don't hurt you, even though I would never do it intentionally. I'm concerned that you might misunderstand me at some point and take offense", because anybody who sets themselves up to be hurt will surely be hurt by anybody. If all you do is think about getting hurt, you're going to get hurt. In fact, you're going to make it happen because you were thinking about it. It's the law of attraction; whatever you think about, you will draw to you.

Your fear will manipulate it into taking place. I didn't say anything, but I shook his hand, loved him, and accepted him where he was. He came to church the next Sunday and we had a guest speaker that happened to be his former pastor that offended him. He looked like somebody was holding a machine gun in his face. All during the service I didn't have a clue what was going on. After the service was over, it took me a while to get to the back. He came up to me and told me the story and how God must have orchestrated him to visit a totally random church after 15 years and send the "offender" as the guest speaker that morning. By the way, that was the first time I had ever had that particular pastor in my pulpit to preach. Praise God, there was a reconciliation between the two men.

WHO'S IN YOUR HOUSE?

Fifteen years of disconnection and offense? This kind of thing happens more than you think, people remain angry for years, and don't care to do anything about it. Meanwhile, it's eating away at their destiny and God-ordained purpose. Many people make these bold statements, saying, *"I'll never trust the pastor again."* And I think, *"Now wait a minute. You'll never a trust a pastor again?"* Come on, you were hurt by one pastor and now you can't trust the hundreds other pastors around you? I hear women say, *"I'll never trust a man again."* Some men say, *"I'll never trust a woman again."* Things happen, people draw these hard-lined, general, broad sweeping conclusions that are designed to bring a slow death. They draw conclusions based on the only way they know how to deal with the pain.

Drawing Conclusions

By drawing conclusions, you miss the joy, destiny, and purpose of God in your life and relationships. Your life is blocked off to any potential relationship. You miss the power of God to bring healing. You miss the connectedness with others that God ordained to take you to the next level. Basically, you miss real life!

In all my years of ministry, I have been hurt by someone who was carrying their own level of pain. Mix that with people who match it with my level of pain and rejection, and you have a recipe for disaster. However, I am not bitter, or closed off and guarded. If I was, I would have been seriously jaded in my motive and heart for ministry. Many pastors hide out in back rooms before and after service solely because they are not going to interact with people and risk that someone will hurt them.

WHO'S IN YOUR HOUSE?

When we choose not to do something God's way, this has horrific consequences. I think back over the years of ministry on the valuable relationships that I cherish and will forever value. It validates the faithfulness of God to us. This is the power of relationships.

You will get hurt. There is no such thing as not getting hurt. However, you are wiser now and you can dare to risk and strategically walk through a relationship by testing it from the front porch, which will always able consistent with His divine purpose. You must dare to risk, with God's help!

CHAPTER 4

THE DEN

THE DEN

As you allow people in your life, some people can be "friends" and be on the front porch. Some people can be friends and be in the formal area. Some people can be friends, but they are formal friends. You can do a lot of Kingdom business and thoroughly enjoy each other as a formal friend. There is nothing wrong with being a formal friend. This is where some are assigned to be in your life.

All friends cannot and should not be intimate friends. It does not work in the Kingdom if everybody is intimate with everybody. I suggest no more than two or three, what if you tried to maintain multiple intimate relationships? You wouldn't have enough time for anything else. You need a smaller amount of people that you are close to because that kind of relationship requires a lot of give and take. You cannot be that to a lot of people, so I believe in the den you can probably count those friends on one hand, but you would not have that many really close friends.

If you are married, your spouse should be your closest intimate friend. To do that, you need to learn how to play and lighten things up a little.

> *The den is where you could go in, kick your shoes off and maybe put something on that is a little more comfortable.*

Everything doesn't have to be so serious. You need to learn how to enjoy life and enjoy one another. Sometimes we get so caught up in bills, work, kids, our homes, and running here and running there that we forget that we are best friends and that we are supposed to be having fun together! You ought to set aside time to play in your relationship, to enjoy the friend that God has allowed you to spend the rest of your life with, and to be an intimate friend with your spouse.

We have used the analogy of the front porch and then we went to the formal area of the house, the formal living and dining rooms, which becomes the next boundary that you create. Then we went to the good ole' southern kitchens. The kitchen was a place where you let your hair down a little and that was where you laughed, ate and stayed up all night, sat around the table but the kitchen was different from the den.

The den is where you could go in, kick your shoes off and maybe put something on that is a little more comfortable. I used to put on a pair of gym shorts and t-shirt to be a little more casual. They know your feet stink, and they know your toes are ugly –

these are the people that you allow into the den of your life. When you allow them into the den, the next level is the bedroom, which is the highest level of intimacy.

God desires that intimate relationship with you. In fact, He designed you and me for that kind of intimacy. God wants us to dwell in His house, but we stay on the front porch. He is calling us in and we, by our own choosing, remain distant from God. God does not want to be your vacation home, he wants to be your dwelling place. He wants you to dwell with him, commune with Him, and experience His glory!

When you go into your house, you do not have any problem knowing where the bedroom is. You normally go to your bedroom to change, prepare, or to find refuge. You and I find that refuge in an intimate relationship with God through Jesus Christ. It's a beautiful and powerful thing to experience.

So now we approach intimacy in close relationships. We are going from casual to close. Christians should be looking for like-minded believers. It does not make sense for Christians to be close friends with non-Christians. You can be friends with non-Christians, but you must have the same vision if you are going to be close to somebody. If you are close to them, you have the same vision for life and share the same values and purpose. Ask yourself; *"Will this person improve on my character? We say that people are like elevators: they take you up; they take you down?"*

I say people will either drag you down or push you on, and no one can stand to be with someone very long that constantly pulls you down. Typically, what happens is you become more like them, instead of them becoming more like you. When you become close to somebody that is not of like mind in the things of God, you become more like them. And when you become more like them, you lose sight of your vision. The problem is that you let it happen in the first place by allowing that person too close in your life.

There is nothing wrong with allowing a non-Christian to be a front porch friend. You can still have fun, still be a witness, still love them with the love of the Lord but you have not allowed them into your life because they do not share the same Godly values. You want to make sure that they add to your character, that they encourage you.

In Proverbs, Chapter 22, verse 24, *"Do not make friends with a hot-tempered man. Do not associate with one easily angered."* If they are easily angered, they are going to be easily angered with you. If they talk about other people around you, they will talk about you when you are not around. If they are easily offended, you do not want them in your den, because they will abort the relationship for no good reason. If they get mad because you do not call to talk, then they do not need to be in a close relationship because they do not understand what a close relationship is really like. You are the one in control!

In the 25th verse, it says, *"If you associate with one easily angered or make friends with a hot tempered man, you may learn his ways and get yourself in snares."* In other words, you will become like him or her. You want to hang around with people who are not like that so that you can be positively influenced and not trapped in their unbalanced emotions.

Probably one of the greatest examples of this is teenagers. Teenagers will hang around with the wrong group for one reason…acceptance. When that happens, they start to take on the personality of their particular group of peers. What happens typically is the teenager start dressing like they dress, acting like they act, seeing the movies that they see, talking like them because they are motivated by the desire to be accepted. In other words, you are willing to invite them into the closest area of your life because you want them to accept you and now, you are not the one setting the boundaries. You have given up your control!

Furthermore, do not look for perfect people. If you are in a relationship with somebody, and you are always wrong and they are always right, something is messed up. If you are going to allow somebody close into your life, they are going to have to know a few intimate details about you, one being that you are not perfect. And vice versa-you are going to have to know that they are not perfect either and you accept one another with your imperfections, and you love each other. The key is that God will always establish something special through true friendships.

Before I get to the dynamics of a close relationship, I want you to see that it is the will of God for you to have friends. So if you have zero friends, you need to call Doctor Phil, call Oprah, call somebody because you need some close friends, and there is some level of dysfunction if that's the case. In all seriousness, just call Jesus, and let God heal you of what has kept you from having close friends because you need to have them. God will love you through difficult people.

Proverbs 17:17 says, *"A friend loves at all times."* This is powerful. *"And a brother is born for adversity."* God will love you and strengthen you through friends. You will become a better person by the people that you hang out with. That is why you carefully choose who you want to be around.

In some cases, the people that you hang out with on Saturday night are not like the people that you are with on Sunday. If that's true, then there is a sign that something is wrong and that you are making choices for the wrong reasons. You need friends that are going to strengthen you in that relationship and help you want to get stronger in your goal, your purpose, and your vision for life. Get wisdom!

You must have wisdom to be able to discern what somebody's motive is in a relationship. If they are in a relationship to "get you fixed" they do not need to be a den friend. They must remain a front porch friend. If they are always picking at your faults and never do any wrong, it's time to readjust their position. People deserve an opportunity to get healed, learn big lessons, and to let God deal with them as a healer. You do not push them out forever, but you are always testing whether or not you allow that person back in. Then, and only then, will you allow them closer in your life.

Now remember that these are not levels you get promoted too. People don't get promoted into the next level. All levels are good, but all levels must be God. If a certain person is on the front porch and that's where God wants him/her, then that place is a perfect God place for them.

In the Old Testament Tabernacle, we talked about the outer core, the inner core, and the Holy of Holies. The outer core is bigger than the inner core and the inner core is bigger than the Holy of Holies. It gets smaller because there are less people allowed into those intimate areas of high trust. This is the kind of person that you would play with or pray with. The den is the place where you have to be yourself.

Dynamics Of A Close Friendship

1. The first dynamic is: *Close friends stay together through highs and lows, sorrows and joys.* Close friends will always hang with you. If you gain 50 pounds, your close friend is going to stick with you. If you start having hormonal issues, your close friends are going to stick with you. If you have experience death or grief or something emotional is going on, the close friends are going to stick with you. They will be there to comfort you and help you along the way. A real friend will listen to you complain even when you are wrong. A real friend will comfort you and encourage you every step of the way. A real friend is committed. They are not a fair-weather friend.

I believe that relationships have seasons. People move away and you lose contact. They are

148

certainly committed because true friendship has no geographical boundaries. Even if you don't talk to them much, you are still connected by God's divine purpose. They are still your friend and you can call or visit them any time, and they will always welcome you. If you have not talked with them in a year, you can talk to them on the phone once and it is like you have not missed any time at all. I understand things like that, but a real friend is going to stick with you through the highs, the lows, the sorrows and the joys. Proverbs 17:17 again says, *"A friend loves at all times and a brother is born of adversity."*

There was a man in a small town that was very well liked by most of the town's people. He was a happy man, and he always made the people around him happy. Everyone knew his name. They enjoyed seeing his smiling face around town. Then, he was in a tragic car accident and was paralyzed from the neck down. People from the town came to visit him in the hospital in large numbers. When he got out of the hospital and was taken home in his permanent wheelchair, the town's people realized that he would be paralyzed for the rest of his life. People went to visit him, but it was not long until they started to fade out of the picture.

You know all how that goes. The real friends are the ones who are still there when everybody else has gone. The real friends are the ones to comfort you three days after your mother has died. Those are the real friends that will stick with you and hang tight with you because they are committed to you as a true friend. Just realize that there will always be the type of "friends" that fade out of the picture for whatever reason. There is no need to judge them and their "lack of commitment." It was not intended for everyone to hang with you all the time, but a close friend will stick with you, be there for you, and love you no matter what. That is exactly what a close friend should do because it shows their genuine love and concern for you. It passes the test of intimacy.

2. The second dynamic of a close friendship is: *close friends are honest even when it is difficult.* Don't allow someone to flatter you in order to get close to you with destructive behavior. In Proverbs 27:6 it says, *"Wounds from a friend can be trusted but an enemy multiplies kisses."* Someone may say, *"You are so sweet! You are so wonderful! You're amazing!"* And then they turn around and stab you right in the back by speaking ill of you or mistreating you. Almost everyone has experienced this type of flattery coming from a selfish, destructive person. All the more reason to exercise discernment from the Holy Spirit. When I see this trait in someone,

WHO'S IN YOUR HOUSE?

I automatically think that they are going to stay on the front porch, because no one can tolerate that kind of inconsistency daily. It's safer for you to love them on the front porch of your life.

On the other hand, it is good to have a trusted friend that will be completely honest with you and you can trust that their agenda is purely out of their love for you. It's great to have someone compliment you, offer encouragement, and speak life into you, but it is also necessary to have someone that will speak truth, even when it might hurt. True friends will lovingly speak truth into your life.

It is also important to mention that people go through things that cause them to become clouded to God's best, and they lean more on their emotions, resulting in unusual behavior. They get further from God and more into themselves. It happened to

Moses, Judas, and even Peter. It can happen to you too.

When it does happen to you, you want someone who will be honest and help you to get back on track. Better for you to trust a friend's correction and be whole, then to reject any truth from another person and allow confusion to take over. The more it takes over, the bigger it gets, and the more control it has over us.

3. The third dynamic is: *a close friend will help you with your spiritual journey.* Close friends almost always share the same vision for life. They need to love God the same as you love Him. Their moral compass and overall character should be close to yours. You can be confident that they will "fan your flame" when it comes to encouraging you on your spiritual journey. They will pray with you and for you.

WHO'S IN YOUR HOUSE?

Sometimes you feel like giving up, and you need someone to encourage you to get back on track. Sometimes the circumstances are overwhelming and things look impossible, and a good friend will stand with you so you can be strong together.

A man came to me one time and wanted an appointment. When the time came for us to meet, we met in my office. We shook hands, we prayed, and I gave him an opportunity to share what was on his heart. He said that he wanted to be to me what Jonathan was to David. I thanked him for his desire to stand with me with such a high level of dedication. However, I was really thinking that we hardly knew each other well enough to trust each other at that level.

David and Jonathan were close and Jonathan left Saul to be closer to David. Saul was jealous of David. The Bible says that their souls were "knitted together." The man said, "I want to be there for you. You are a man after God's own heart. I want to help you in every way that I can." He offered to wash my car, pick up my dry-cleaning, and cut my grass. I was a little uncomfortable at his suggestions because I just wasn't used to that type of thing. I didn't commit either way. I just thanked him, and he left. About four weeks later, I was in the pulpit and I corrected his wife when she tried to speak out in the middle of the service. I simply asked her not speak at that particular time. Well, as you could guess, she got offended, and two days later, he was not my "Jonathon" anymore.

I learned was that he never was capable of that in the first place. He said that he wanted to be, but he did not have the character. If you say you are going to commit to somebody to be a faithful friend, do so with a level of dedication and commitment to them. This man wanted to commit, but he wanted it on his terms, not on the terms of the relationship. I'm convinced he was completely unaware of his impure heart and motive. That is the problem you have with a lot of relationships, people running other agendas, and quite possibly in complete denial. Relationships like that are one-sided and totally on their terms. That is exactly why you have to learn to set boundaries and be completely in control of what you where you allow people in the relationship.

David and Jonathan were close and David had become popular. The people were singing, "Saul has killed his thousands and David his ten thousands." Saul was jealous of David. In first Samuel 18:1, *"The soul of Jonathan was knit to the soul of David and Jonathan loved him as his own soul."* Verse three says, *"Then Jonathan and David made a covenant because he loved him as his own soul."*

Jonathan was so committed to David that in the deepest, darkest, most difficult times in his life, he was there to help David find his strength in God. If you do not have a friend like that, God wants to send that kind of friend to you. Please understand that we are talking about a close, intimate friend. We are not talking about front porch friends; this is more like a den friend or a bedroom friend. You can't have multiple, close, intimate friends. I have many "good friends" but they are not intimate friends. We still have fun, laugh, and pray together, and we cherish the friendship. It's not an insult to someone to be your "friend" but not be a true, intimate friend. You don't graduate in this model of relationships. You simply allow people closer based on their ability to prove themselves over time. Please

> *The closer people get, the more it hurts when they betray you. If they betray the friendship from the front porch, you have not lost much.*

don't look at it like a disappointment if things don't work out. It is more about celebrating where you are and being wise in the things of life, so that you are not easily.

The closer people get, the more it hurts when they betray you. If they betray the friendship from the front porch, you have not lost much. If they betray the friendship from the formal area, you have not lost much. If they betray the friendship from the kitchen, you are losing a little, but you are still in a position where it is not going to hurt as bad. But if you let them into the den and they betray the friendship, you have lost a lot because they know a lot about you. And now their intentions are not pure and it will work against you. So be wise.

Once, I visited a lady in the hospital and she had a lot of friends in the room with her, along with a few family members. The room was packed. There was also a large number of people in the waiting room. She obviously had a huge support group. I went in, prayed with her, talked to her about her surgery a little bit and she thanked me for being there. We chatted in the room a few more minutes. Some of them I did not even know.

When I left, a couple of her friends who were in the hospital room, followed me out. As we walked into the hallway, this is what they said to me, "Pastor, we appreciate your being here. We know you are very busy, and we just want you to know that we have her covered. We will take care of her and be there through this stay at the hospital and when she goes home." I responded, "Well that is nice that she has you all here to help her, pray with her and provide the necessary support. I will keep a check on her." I walked away, happy knowing that she had such a support group around her that she had people who were actually taking care of her and meeting her needs. That is what close friends do.

So, if you invite someone to attend church with you, there's a good possibility that, if your church is sensitive to the leading of the Holy Spirit and God's Presence, that your guest is going to receive some level of healing from being there with you. I cannot tell you how many e-mails, letters and phone calls I receive from people who say that they were going through a difficult time in their life, or they had been depressed or discouraged, and just wanted to give up, and miraculously they began to feel God's hand of healing.

This scenario is repeated over and over in our church. It happens, because somebody cared enough to say, "Would you go to church with me Sunday?" They receive the best of God's healing presence and touch. If they walk out of that service knowing how much Jesus loves them, they have received sustenance. You probably knew they needed the ministry, which was why you invited them in the first place.

True friends care about you and will encourage you to grow, trust the process, keep moving, and don't look back. They will encourage you to get closer to God and discover that He really does care about you and has a divine purpose you.

4. The fourth dynamic is – *to have a close friend is to be a close friend.* You cannot have a den friend and be a kitchen friend. Proverb 18:24 says, *"A man of many companions may come to ruin but there is a friend who sticks closer than a brother."* True, intimate friends are hard to find. Everyone needs somebody who will stand with you, no matter what happens. This type of friend will stick with you even when you struggle, and don't feel strong. Have you ever known someone and hoped they could possibly become a true intimate friend, yet you realized after a while that it could never work? Don't be discouraged because God has given you the wisdom to be able to discern these things enough to set the right boundaries. Instead of being discouraged, you should feel blessed that God has given you discernment that will help you to avoid a different kind of heartache later.

Isn't it true that when you reach a certain age, society has already pre-determined certain things that should have taken place by now? Sometimes they will think, *"Shouldn't you be married by now at your age? Is there some reason you're not?"* I like it when confident people respond, *"There is nothing wrong. I am just being wise. God hasn't sent the right person yet. I'm not going to be moved by world expectations if God tells me to wait."* In other words, *"I am not looking. God is going to send them to me."* Desperation is never a good motivator for close, intimate, and trusting relationships. Relationships that happen like that are usually one-sided and unhealthy. To have a close friend is to be a close friend. Even when they are difficult to find, God will bring them into your life.

5. The fifth dynamic is–*close friends should model a relationship with Jesus Christ.* A close friend should be a model of Christ. You should be a model of Christ to the people around you. The familiar saying is, "You're the only Jesus some will ever see." Look what God has done for you besides saving you and giving you eternal and everlasting life! Has He been faithful to you? Has He strengthened you over and over? Has He been there through all of your crazy stuff? Is He committed to you for life? The answer is a resounding…YES! That is the kind of friend He is to you. That is the kind of friend you should be to Him and to others. He has been there for you, you ought to be faithful to Him. If you are going to be a friend, then model that kind of friendship. I don't know about you but I am grateful for the wonderful friends in my life that stood by me when I didn't deserve it, and they loved me unconditionally, encouraged me, prayed for and with me, and made lots of sacrifices when I wasn't much of a friend to them at the time, and had nothing at the time to give.

This is where you need maturity, seasoning, and wisdom in a friend. You know that God loves you, right? Out of His love for you, He wants to commune with you and you with Him. You should decide that you are not going to be a front porch friend to God. What kind of a friend are you to those you are intimate with? Are you a giving friend who sacrifices for the sake of the good of the other person? Would you consider walking out on them if they become too much for you? Are you a friend that remains steadfast even when things do not go your way? One thing I have learned in relationships is that it's "give and take", but mostly "give."

In Ecclesiastes 4:9 it says, *"Two are better than one because they have a good return for their work."* Then it says in verse ten, *"If one falls down, his friend can help him up but pity the man who falls and has no one to help him up."* How many is this talking about? Two! In verse eleven, *"Also if two lie down together they will keep warm, but how can one keep warm alone?"* How many is this talking about? Two! In Verse twelve, *"The one may be overpowered. Two can defend themselves."* Again, how many is this talking about? Two! It never was intended for you to do it alone.

In verse 12 it says, *"A cord of three strands is not quickly broken."* Where did the third strand come from? I believe the third strand is God. If you have a friend and you share the same vision and life, God should be at the center of that friendship because a three stranded cord is not quickly broken. In other words, it is you, that friend, and God intertwined to be strengthened to sustain that friendship.

We all have friends who have not withstood the test. Give it to God. You may be thinking, *"Well, that's easy for you to say."* Trust me I know what I am talking about and I am not trying to be insensitive. I am only trying to say that God never intended for you to always remain in pain because He is a healer. That is one reason He sent Jesus-so you could be healed. Your healing may not take place until you let go of something. If you are hurt by somebody, it will affect every relationship that you enter from now on. Right now, you need to let God heal you, so you can wisely discern all current and future relationships. Otherwise, everything ahead of you will become clouded and jaded by existing, unresolved, unhealed pain.

There are people who get married simply because they are lonely. Of course, they wouldn't admit it, and that is the wrong reason to get married. There are people who enter into friendships out of a "need" for acceptance and approval, when they should first be validated by God. These and many others are wrong reasons to enter a relationship. All we need to do is to follow the truth (John 8:32). You want to make sure your heart is pure so that you allow the right people into your life and in the right kind of Godly, God-ordained relationships. If you have money and somebody is your close friend, you need to find out if they want to be friends because you have money. You do not want a friend who is going to be friend for what he can get out of you. Otherwise, this relationship will suck the life out of you that God wants to keep in you.

Exercise Godly discernment. If you have been hurt, let God heal you and let Him bring you to a place where you can say, "I want my spouse to be my best friend." Repeat that over and over until you have the intent in your heart to be bonded and united with the person that is already "one" with you.

God is first, but my spouse is my best friend. You need to determine that throughout all your relationships. If you are not married, you want your future spouse to be your best friend, who is capable of giving and receiving love in a lasting, healthy relationship. You want somebody who is going to hang with you, when things don't always work out for the best, someone who won't threaten to walk out on you when you struggle. Perhaps I am describing your spouse. If not, you need to develop this the same way you develop your relationship with God.

To have God as a friend is to be a friend. To have a spouse as a friend is to be a friend. Become that friend to your spouse and love them unconditionally. After all, God loves us regardless of what we do, right? So we love our spouses regardless of what they do to us, because we are true friends. *"It does not matter what you do, you are my friend. It does not matter what you do not do, you are my friend."* No matter what, I am still my wife's friend. If I do not pick up my dirty clothes, I am still her friend. If I don't perform perfectly, we are still friends.

God wants you to develop your relationship with Him. He wants to dwell with you. When I come home from work, I walk into the house and say, "I cannot wait to change clothes get into something more comfortable, and just kick back and relax, work around the house, and spend time with my family." Do you do that? Notice that we don't stop and analyze every room before we go to the bedroom to change into something more comfortable. That's because you have access to your bedroom and you know exactly where it is.

Do you know it's just that easy with God? In your relationship with God, if you are on the front porch, now it's time to start moving into intimacy with Him. Start going into that dwelling place with Him and dwell with Him in an intimate relationship. Say to God, "You have been so faithful to me. You have loved me when I didn't deserve it. You have blessed me when I didn't deserve it. God, I am sticking with you all the way!"

I have given you a lot of different scenarios, and of course, there are many more situations. However, the bottom line is when we get hurt we start to build walls to prevent it from every happening to us again. The only problem is that some of those walls are unnecessary and detrimental. Perhaps you are in a situation now where you really want the wisdom of God because it looks good, it looks right, and you want His wisdom. God will give it to you because He wants you to have good, healthy friendships. He wants you to have people in your life that are close, for the purpose of greater power for His kingdom advancement.

Maybe you are struggling in your marriage and you and your spouse have become very distant and disconnected. Your spouse is your best friend. You should sit down with them and say, "You are my friend, my best friend in the whole world. I want to be with you, enjoy life together, and share our pains and hurts together." Begin to allow God to do what it is He needs to do through you for that to happen. Be that kind of friend no matter what your spouse does.

I suggest that you not pray for God to change your spouse; instead, pray that God will change you so that you can be the friend that he or she needs that loves them and stays connected regardless of whether they are weak or strong. There are a lot of potentially different things that can be going on in a person, but God can heal them of anything. He just might want you to play a role by offering unconditional love.

CHAPTER 5

THE BEDROOM

THE BEDROOM

As stated previously, if you are married, your spouse should be your closest friend. Learn how to be a close, Godly friend with your spouse. You should learn how to love unconditionally, forgive quickly, and be the friend to them you would like for them to be to you. Learn how to enjoy God, life, and one another. Sometimes we get so caught up in bills and work and kids and house and running here and running there that we forget that we are best friends and that we are supposed to be enjoying life together! So you ought to set aside time to be together away, to enjoy the friend that God has allowed you to spend the rest of your life with, and to be a close friend to them. Be a true intimate friend with your spouse.

WHO'S IN YOUR HOUSE?

When you have allowed someone into the den of your life, the next level is the bedroom. Take all the sexual overtones out. This level of bedroom intimacy that we have with our spouse, God, and maybe one other same-sex friend is valuable and extremely healthy for any person desiring a pure, whole life. God wants an intimate relationship with you and He wants some of your relationships to model that.

God wants us to dwell in His house, with Him, but so often we stay on the front porch. Even though He is calling us in, we, by our own choosing stay away from Him. God does not want to be your vacation home. He wants you to dwell with Him.

As we go through this last chapter in this book on relationships, you notice that we have been talking about setting the right kind of boundaries in relationships and how important it is to be able to put relationships to the test before you allow people too closely into your life. You can be more in control of relationships and how they should be assessed.

> *Make sure that you understand the dynamic as you allow people to come into your life in friendships and relationships.*

God never intended for you to have a deep intimate relationship with everybody. You can have many different kinds of relationships that can be surface relationships, casual friendships, good friendships, and stronger friendships. They will not all be intimate.

First, God wants you to have an intimate relationship with Him. I want you to try to block out of your mind the idea of "graduating" from one level to another in these relationships. You do not "graduate" from the front porch, into the foyer, into the formal area, into the kitchen, into the den and then into the bedroom. Make sure that you understand the dynamic as you allow people to come into your life in friendships and relationships.

A lot of people get hurt because they allow people in too quickly, too "close" and set themselves up to get hurt in those relationships. It's easy to blame them and say, "Well, why did they do this to me? Why did they turn their back on me? Why did they stab me in the back?" Perhaps you did not assess that person from a healthy frame of reference when it comes to relationships and friendships. You didn't put that relationship to the test. The end result is that a lot of people get hurt and when they get hurt, they become very guarded. Truly, there are people who have been around for many years and have not had healthy relationships because they have been so guarded. They have built fortresses around them to protect them from ever being hurt again. This is a serious issue and void of God's purpose to use us as examples of His love to the world. God's intent is that you would have many relationships and that His power would flow through each of these relationships to bring healing, and examples of His love and faithfulness.

Some people believe others can be changed solely from the pulpits of churches around the world. Rather, the best way for the world to transformed for God is from the seats of those churches, by the people who have a healthy, intimate relationship with God, and they can model it to others daily.

We need to understand that we touch people's lives by what we say and who we are. We touch them by the relationships or the connection that we have with Him. So, it is very critical that we understand the Godly, Kingdom value of our being in relationships. We must be in relationships with the people around us, at work, at church, and so forth. But everything flows out of a pure, healthy, relationship with God. Many people will read this and not understand those words, "relationship with God."

Many people do not understand how to have a relationship with God. The Apostle Paul said, "*That I may know Christ.*" Yes, he wanted to "know" Christ, yet most people think he is referring to some kind of a surface knowledge of Christ. The word, "know," in that scripture comes from the same word that was used for intimate relationships. It is a high level of intimacy. So, what he really said was, "I want to *know* Christ in an intimate way." The Bible says that, "*Mary knew no man.*" And what that means is that she had not been intimate with a man. So, when Paul said, "*I want to know Christ,*" what he said was, "I want to know Christ in an intimate way. I want to know Him in the fellowship of his sufferings. I want to know Christ in every way that I can." You and I have to *know* Christ.

To know Him is to be intimate with Him. When you use the word "intimate," people just get all kind of inappropriate things twisted in their heads. However, I won't avoid this powerful word because the world has limited it to sexual intimacy. Let's come back to the power of what it really means that goes way beyond a physical, sexual connection. In marriage, physical and sexual intimacy is powerful and Godly.

If you have a good, healthy, intimate relationship with Christ, every other relationship will be right and healthy in your life. Conversely, if you do not have a good relationship with Christ, every other relationship will be affected negatively. If you do not have a solid relationship with Jesus, then you are running like an airplane without an instrument panel. You don't have any direction or focus. You are moving fast, but you just don't know where you are going or where you are going to end up. When you have an intimate relationship with Christ, there is more understanding in the relationships than you will have with others.

As you develop in your relationships, with God as the foundation, He gives you the wisdom to discern -- because there is a lot going on out there in this crazy world. There are people who have impure agendas and are not even aware that they are operating emotionally, unhealthy, and out of balance. There are people who know they have agendas, but do not care. There are also people out there who are pure, and they work constantly on keeping their heart and life pure. You must be able to discern what is pure and right, and what is not, because you do not want to let someone with an agenda in too closely into your life. You must be the one who draws the boundaries. You have to be the one who decides how close you let people get to you, so that you may avoid being wounded and "hurt" so much, or even derailed.

Now this doesn't mean that you will never be hurt. You will be hurt, but you have to dare to risk. If you walk through something with wisdom, then you are taking a risk knowing that you might get hurt. When you choose to take that risk, you know that that the grace of God is going to cover you. Certain people will talk about you in a negative light. People will do things behind your back. But, if those people are on the front porch when they say or do something, it is a lot different than if they were in the bedroom of your life. By the time you let them into that intimate area, you want to be sure that they have passed all the tests. It is so much more dangerous, and hurts so much more, when betrayals start to happen in the intimate areas of your life, rather than when they

occur on the front porch.

Remember, God has passed all the tests! He

does not have to pass any test to be in an intimate

relationship with you. He gave His only Son to die for

our sins. God loves us unconditionally. He always

has; He always will. It doesn't matter what you do; it

doesn't matter where you have been; it doesn't matter

what you have done. *God loves you unconditionally*.

So, God has passed all the tests. God loved you

when you were not even around. God loved you when

you were so far away from Him that you did not know

His name. He still loved you. You know that God

passed all the tests because you know that when you

have strayed from God and then returned into His

presence, He greeted you like the Father did the

prodigal son. He welcomed you with open arms. He

had a big party and a big celebration and He said, "Thank God my child is home."

God desires an intimate relationship with you and God wants you to be in healthy relationships with other people. That is why God wants us to be in fellowship.

In I John 1:3 it says, *"We proclaim to you what we have seen and heard so that you also may have fellowship with us and our fellowship is with the Father and with his Son Jesus Christ."* Verse 7 says, *"But if we walk in the light as He is in the light, we have fellowship with one another and the blood of Jesus, His son, purifies us from all sin."* Fellowship with one another and fellowship with Christ is foundational for all relationships.

We have to have the right kind of fellowship and relationship with Christ. When you have the right kind of relationship with God, everything else falls into place. You have to have that intimate relationship with God through Jesus Christ, on which you have built everything else. Understand today that God wants to have a relationship with you, the question remains, do you want to have a relationship with Him? A relationship with God is a choice and an act of your will. That is why you must make the choice to know that God not only created us for fellowship, but God put the desire in you to have fellowship with Him. Let's go one step further. He not only put the desire in you; He put the power in you to have fellowship with Him so that when the enemy wants you to "hang out" with him, you have the grace, which is the power and the desire, to have fellowship with the Father.

It is important to God that we are in communion with Him. We cannot know the will of God unless we are in fellowship. You can follow certain principles in the Word and not be in intimate relationship with Him, but you cannot know the will of God unless you are in true fellowship and communion. People want blessings, protection, and strength, but they do not have communion with God. They want direction and purpose, but yet they are not in fellowship with God. We must be in fellowship with Him to know His will and purpose.

So, what people in the church often think is, "Well, since I am a Christian, I must automatically have fellowship with God." Not necessarily. God wants to have fellowship with you, but it is up to you to choose if you want to have fellowship with Him. You can call yourself a Christian and not be in relationship with Him.

If I went for days or weeks without speaking to my wife, I would have a relationship with her, but not intimate fellowship. I am still her husband, but something is wrong. We are not communing together.

So, we must continue to work and develop that kind of relationship.

It is same thing with God. We become so religious that we forget to have fellowship. We follow all of the laws, but we forget to develop our fellowship and our intimacy with God. We practice and sing the songs, but we are not reading our Bibles; we are not praying; we are not communicating; we are not worshiping God out of intimacy. We're acting religious, but we are not following God. The Israelites practiced the law, kept the sacrifices, honored the feast days and followed all of the religious requirements. What did God do? He judged them.

Why did He judge them? Because they forsook their relationship with Him. Matthew 15:8 says, *"These people honor me with their lips but their hearts are far from me. They worship me in vain.*

Their teachings are but rules taught by men." Now, if our worship is "religious," it is not going to work.

If your relationship with your wife or husband is in name only, there is no intimacy. You are more like a robot than a Godly human. You are in trouble and what that relationship needs is intimacy. It needs all the dynamics of intimacy because you have invited one another into each other's life. In marriages, occasionally, somebody gets hurt or offended. Things happen that interrupt the normal flow of life and the next thing you know distance is created between the two of you. Intimacy is gone and everybody is just going through the motions of marriage. Because I'm offended or mad, I will remain disconnected until you change. Have you ever tried that? How did it work out? It never works out, because it's the wrong thing to do and never honors God. The words "I love you" do not mean what they used to mean. The words

WHO'S IN YOUR HOUSE?

"You are the most important person in my life" do not mean what they used to mean.

As a pastor, when I perform a marriage ceremony, and watch the wedding party, in my mind, I go right back to my wedding day when I saw my wife come down that aisle. No bride looks as good as mine did on that wedding day! My mind constantly goes back to that day and it matches with her inner beauty today. That kind of intimacy has to be developed; it has to be worked on. There are certain things you have to sacrifice and certain things you have to give up.

We are talking about intimacy on a natural, earthy level, with a human, but we are also talking about intimacy with our Heavenly Father. I value my intimate relationship with Him. That means God is telling me what to correct in my life. He is continuously telling me how to fix certain things in my life so that when I enter into earthly relationships, He can use me as a pure vessel and not a person that has a lot of impure agendas. I want to model the same intimacy that I have with God in my earthly relationships. I want to model that intimacy with my wife, but I must have a real relationship with Him first.

Where there is intimacy, there is vulnerability. There are people who see things about you that nobody else has seen. Those are people who know you snore all night long, loud enough to disturb the neighbors. They know when you are moody. They know you have a temper. They know those little quirks about you, and love you, because we are all a work in progress. God knows every one of those things about you and more and He is patient with you as you grow, mature, and change out of some of your old fleshly ways and habits.

WHO'S IN YOUR HOUSE?

You are very vulnerable to those in the den and bedroom of your life. You do not want to be vulnerable to somebody who is a gossip or who has this hidden desire to destroy your life. Logically, you do not want them to know intimate things about you if they are going to use those things against you. How many times have you let somebody in too quickly, too closely, you revealed yourself, and then they used it against you in some way? That hurts. It is really painful when that kind of thing happens to us.

So the idea here is that I am vulnerable, I am exposed, and God is telling me that I am not supposed to be alone. At His direction, I have to risk making myself vulnerable in certain relationships. That means becoming attached or joined together. The Bible says that the two come together as one.

All things are going to bring us closer together. The mountains that we climb and valleys we forge through in our relationships are going to bring us closer together. The struggles and the celebrations are going to bring us closer together because I am putting aside my fear of exposure and I am opening myself up to the person that I am connected to and to God. We open ourselves up to the person because we're overcoming the fear of being known, being found out. That is why intimacy is so important. Christ must be at the center of it all. We must have an intimate relationship with Jesus before anything else can be built.

John 15:15 says, *"I no longer call you servants because a servant does not know his master's business. Instead I have called you friends for everything that I learned from my father I have made known to you."* Romans 8 says that we are sons of God. In I John 3, it says we are children of God.

WHO'S IN YOUR HOUSE?

Hebrews 2:11 says that we are called His brethren.

John 15 refers to us as His sheep.

> **If you are going to act like the devil, then people are going to think your father is the devil.**

There is this place in God where we are His sons, His children, His brethren, His sheep and that we are in fellowship. John 15:15 says that we are friends, but it is compared to being servants. Verse 14 says, *"You are my friend if you do what I command."* In other words, we are the friends of God if we pass the test. God is not interested in our being fickle in our friendship with Him. For us to be friends with God, we must be in right relationship with him.

I John 3:9 and 10 says, *"No one who was born of God will continue to sin because God's seed remains in him. He cannot go on sinning because he has been born of God. This is how we know who the children of God are and who the children of the devil are. Anyone who does not do what is right is not a child of God, nor anyone who does not love his brother."* People say, "Well that is interesting because that is saying that they are no longer the child," but what it is really saying is you are not acting like you know your last name.

My children have my last name, but if they ever do anything that is inconsistent with our family philosophy, they are still my children; they are just not acting like it. What we have here is God's kids who are not acting like God's kids. We have people in the church who are not acting like children of God. People who call themselves Christians but are not acting like children of God. People who are living one way one day and another way the next day. And God says, "You are not acting like my kids."

WHO'S IN YOUR HOUSE?

If you are going to act like the devil, then people are going to think your father is the devil. In fact, your father might be the devil and you don't even know it. My dad, used to tell us all the time when we went out as teenagers, "Remember your last name." I used to think when he said that, "Remember my last name? I do not have any problem remembering my last name." I remember he also said, "You need to remember that your last name is my last name." He was saying, "You represent my name." So, remember, when you and I are in out our relationships, we represent His Name. We represent Christ in everything that we do.

Here are some of the dynamics of intimate relationships:

- **Intimate relationships always model the example of Christ.**

Every natural relationship you have needs to be based on your relationship with Christ, modeled after Him, or that relationship will never maintain a healthy standard. If you make sure that you are in right relationship with God, your other relationships can be healthy. For example, I am in intimate relationship with my wife. If my relationship with God suddenly becomes unhealthy in some way, it is going to negatively impact my relationship with her. When my relationship with God slips, I may become very self-centered. When you become selfish in a marriage, you impact the marriage with a cloud of impurity that will grow into a diseased relationship.

Perhaps I am bitter about something that God has or has not done and, as a result, I am distracted because I haven't given it up to God. My mind and thoughts are messed up. My motives are impure and now it gets translated into my relationship with my wife. I would think, "Well, if she does not do for me, then I am not going to do for her" or "Well I am just going to say back to her what she said to me." The next thing you know (and this happens all the time in marriages), there is an unhealthy seed in the marriage. It grows a little at a time, but soon enough, you have a whole yard of weeds and you won't connect to where they came from. What you need is some good Holy Spirit weed killer to come in and kill it all! Zap it and pull it out by the roots. Make sure that it is no longer affecting the relationship because it is making the relationship look pretty trashy—wives are talking about their husbands; husbands are talking about their wives and it is not right. It all stems from the fact that you are not in right relationship with the Father, and it doesn't honor God. Get in right relationship with God and God will help you get in right relationship with your spouse.

- **Intimate relationships are based on giving, and expecting nothing in return.**

I was sharing these points with my wife and she suggested, "And you lay down your expectations." And I said, "Oh that's good." You lay down your expectations because when you are in an intimate relationship with somebody, there are no expectations. You lay them down. Say to your spouse in your heart, "You do not have to do for me. If you never do anything, I still love you." John 17:2 says, *"For you granted him authority over all people that he might give eternal life to all those you have given him."* Verse 6 says, *"I have revealed you to those whom you gave me out of the world. They were*

yours. You gave them to me and they have obeyed

your word. Now they know that everything that you

have given me comes from you for I gave them the

words you gave me and they accepted me. They

knew with certainty that I came from you and they

believed that you sent me." Verse 24 says, *"Father, I*

want those you have given me to be with me where I

am and to see my glory, the glory you have given me

because you loved me before the creation of the

world."

It is all based on giving and expecting

absolutely nothing in return. The word "give" is used

18 times in John Chapter 17. Swapping is not giving.

"Tit for tat" is not giving. "You do for me I will do for

you" is not giving. That is playing games and if you

bring games into your marriage, your marriage will

turn into a disastrous event with no intimacy. Take

games and game playing out of your relationships all together.

"He did not speak to me when he came in; I am not going to speak to him when he comes in. She did not cook me dinner; I am not going to pick up my underwear off the floor. She burned supper; I am not going to cut the grass." It goes on and on with the game playing. He or she did this, so I am going to do this. Get rid of the games. Pull it up by the roots. They are weeds that will affect what God is doing in your life. Lay down your expectations and give, regardless.

That's what intimate relationships are about. Give no matter what, expecting nothing in return. That is exactly what God did when He gave us his Son. He gave, expecting nothing in return and it is up to us to choose to follow what he has given.

- **Intimate relationships are based on discernment and knowledge.**

John 17:17 says, *"Sanctify them by the truth. Your word is truth."* Make sure you know the Word of God and know the truth of God's word. I happened to catch the news one morning when they had a segment with a psycho-analyst on who was talking about stalkers--what stalkers do and why they stalk Hollywood actors and actresses and so forth. The reporter got my attention when she said that people today actually fall "in love" with a picture. They fall "in love" with an actress or an actor; somebody they have never seen, never spoken with. They are "in love" with that person. Their definition of love is so distorted that they do not know what love means.

In other words, they do not know the truth. They have created their own truth and their own belief that they really love somebody they have never seen

200

or spoken with in person. People today are marrying for lust and not for love. Jesus knew the Father intimately. To know love is to experience it in the right way.

- **Intimate relationships quickly clear away unhealthy agendas.**

If you are in an intimate relationship with God, you will deal with agendas quicker. If you are not in an intimate relationship with God, you are not as willing to expose yourself, so you will hold onto your agendas and mask them. When you come into intimate relationship with God, you must recognize your agendas and be willing to get rid of them. You have to be totally honest with yourself and your growth process. Isaiah 29:13 says, *"These people come near to me with their mouth and they honor me with their lips, but their hearts are far from me. Their worship of me is made up only of rules taught by men."* So if you continue unhealthy agendas, they will bog down or destroy relationships. If you have misunderstandings that are allowed to continue and there is a lack of honesty, your relationship is going to bog down. You need to talk about those things. Communication is such an important part of genuine relationship.

- **Intimate relationships require voluntary, regular, and ongoing conversation.**

If you are not talking together, then you are not walking together. You must have healthy conversation. We get so busy with everything. We get up in the morning, we sleep late just in time to get ready quickly, jump in the car, and race to work. We go to school, chasing the school bus down the street, get on the school bus, and zoom to school. Then we zoom to work, go through all of our daily activities, zoom home, sit down, and eat. We zoom to the soccer field or the football field and the next thing you know it's 9 or 10 p.m. It is time to get ready for bed. So you go to bed and get up and do the same things the next morning. You are so tired, that you have not even had conversation with the person in bed with you. It is more like, "How did your day go?" "Fine. How did your day go?" "Fine." "We will talk tomorrow." No conversation. Tomorrow, you get up and go through the same thing.

The next thing you know, somebody in the relationship is saying, "We haven't spent much time together. We have been so busy." What happens is you have not had enough conversations to connect to the needs of the other person. You have not been talking. Take the time. Turn the "devil vision" off and talk. The TV is not a communication device. It is a one-way brain-drain ticket. Turn it off and say, "Let's talk. Just you and me. Let's go outside and have some intimate fellowship."

Just talk! Get in the car and go do something but have conversation. The same thing happens in our relationship with God. We take our Bibles, we look at them on Sunday, we put them down on Sunday night and we say, "I'm going to get to it. I'm going to get to it. I'm going to get to it." Next Sunday morning, your Bible is in the same spot with the same papers in it from last Sunday. The pages have not been touched. Remember the song by Larnelle Harris where he sang the words of Jesus saying, "I miss my time with you. Those moments together." You see, your spouse would say that; why don't you hear God saying that? God longs for intimacy with us. If you are not talking to Him, He is missing His time with you. If I am not talking to my wife, I do not have an intimate relationship with her. It is not healthy. We should be talking and having fun together.

- ## Intimate relationships depend on repentance and forgiveness.

When you are in an intimate relationship with somebody, that person has a right to mess up, they have a right to repent for it, and they also have a right to be forgiven. *"For God so loved the world that He gave His only begotten Son that whosoever believes in Him would not perish but have everlasting life."* God loves us, but pride is the enemy of a good relationship. If we become so proud in our own issues and our own things, that we are unwilling to admit that we are doing anything wrong, then you just allowed an enemy into the camp. If you allowed it to stay, it will heap destruction upon your camp. Do not let the enemy in; kick the enemy out. Do not let pride in. Make sure you repent.

Let me address the men for a minute. Gentlemen, it takes a real man to admit when we are wrong. Guys are so tough and so strong that it is just hard to admit that we make any mistakes, but you need to admit when you are wrong.

Ladies, let your husbands lead. You must be willing to repent. You have to be willing to say, "Look, I have not been letting you do this." Men, you have to be honest and say, "I need to apologize. I have been a fool. I haven't taken you out in six months because I have lost focus and you are more important to me than anything."

- **Intimate relationships can only survive and thrive where there is harmony.**

If somebody is in the formal area of your life and you find out that they are not on the same page as you are, it is not too bad. But, if they are in the bedroom of your life and they are not on the same page, you have a problem. Intimate relationships can only thrive where you are in harmony and agreement with the same vision.

If you are single, do not even think about marrying a non-Christian. First of all, you are unequally yoked with that person and that is not consistent with God's best for you. Secondly, you have different visions. If I had a quarter for every time somebody said to me, "I will change the person after we get married," I would be a rich man. You cannot change a person after you marry them. In fact, in most cases, they change you. You become someone you said you would never become. Make sure you allow God to send you somebody who is on the same page and has the same vision for life and God. Test the relationship. If they are not a Christian, say "No thanks" because there is no way they are going to be on the same page with you. You are going to get up on Sunday morning and they are going to say, "I want to stay in the bed. I need to cut grass. I want to go to the ballgame." And you are going to say, "Well I guess I'll go by myself." And you cannot do that. You must be on the same page.

If you are already married and not on the same page, pray for them, model Christ to them, love unconditionally, and share your heart's desire that the two of you move forward together with the same heart and mind. Talk about how important it is that God has to be first. If He's not first in the life of your spouse, make sure that you keep Him first in your life, at all times, so that you can model God's love toward your spouse.

God wants you to have an intimate relationship with Him. Everybody is a friend, even our enemies. We are still friends with people who come into our lives and then stab us in the back. It's all about boundaries! Where have you not drawn the boundary correctly, and allowed them into an area of your life where they shouldn't be?

Conclusion

As Christians, we are friends to each other and we are friends of God. We believe in God's hand over our lives and we have intimacy with Christ. But to have intimacy with Christ means we should start to act like Him. I want to ask you this: Are you acting like you are the son or daughter of the King?

WHO'S IN YOUR HOUSE?

In other words, if someone saw you in the street would they say, "I know who their father is." Or would they see you in the street and misidentify your father because you are acting like the son or daughter of someone else? So you need to know the answer to this question, because all of your other relationships flow out of your intimacy with God. Religious exercise will never satisfy in this day and age.

Read John 15:16. If you are in intimate relationship with God, your prayers get answered. Do you know why? Because you do not ask amiss. You are asking out of the intimacy that you have one with another. When you are in right relationship with God, your asking is consistent with your relationship with Him. When you ask out of emotion, you are usually asking out of fear. Make sure you're hitting the mark when you ask anything of God.

The only way you can hit the mark is to be in the right relationship with Him. It is not complicated. You have to be in the right relationship with a loving God who loves you more than you can imagine. He has an incredible purpose for your life that involves the joy and blessing of healthy relationships and the lessons from unhealthy relationships. In all of it, God's wants you to be blessed and protected from unnecessary harm.

ABOUT THE AUTHOR

Pastor Fritz Musser is the Apostle and Senior Pastor of Tabernacle International Church, a church with a uniquely diverse congregation with over 50 nations represented each week in worship services. His direct, positive, yet humorous style allows him to present sensitive and powerful life principles in a highly effective manner. His teaching is both Biblically rich and practically relevant for daily life challenges. One of his strongest passions is helping people get to the next level in their life and relationship with God. He and his wife Lisa provide leadership for their local congregation, as well as dozens of other churches and ministries, pastors and leaders, locally and around the world.

Follow Fritz@

Facebook:
https://www.facebook.com/bishopfritz.musser

And Follow his Church:

TABERNACLE INTERNATIONAL CHURCH

Tabernacle Facebook page:
https://www.facebook.com/tabernacleinternational

www.cosbymediaproductions.com

Made in the USA
Columbia, SC
14 December 2018